FOOTBALL

ANYTHING

HOW FOOTBALL HAS BROUGHT OUT THE WORST IN SO MANY FOR THE SPORT THEY "LOVE"

CHRIS ROBERTS

CONTENTS

PART I- WIN AT ALL COSTS

PART II- GREED

<u>ACHKNOWLEDGEMENTS</u>

This book is for all my family who have supported me over the last two years. Especially my fiancée Rachel, who unfortunately must put up with the worst of me daily, as I fight my constant battle. For my two little boys who mean more to me than anything in the whole world and are my shining light on my darkest days. For all my friends who have been there throughout. To Sean's Place for their support and care this past year. Anyone who is suffering depression or feeling down, don't give up.

But most importantly my dad. I love you more than any words can ever describe Christie; I hope I'm doing you proud every day. I hope I can be half the dad you were to me for Zac and Myles.

Introduction

'Some people believe football is a matter of life and death, I am very disappointed with that attitude. I can assure you it is much, much more important than that. '

Bill Shankly OBE, Former Liverpool Manager

Writing a book was something that had never crossed my mind. The thought first came about when I was speaking to a friend in work, who was writing his own book. Seeing his enthusiasm for it and the joy it brought to him made me think this could be a good thing to do. A few weeks later, he sent a draft copy of a chapter of his book into our work WhatsApp group. I read through it and was seriously impressed with the chapter itself, but what interested me about it was in the chapter he had put brackets where he still needed to find references to support what he was writing about. I spent the next hour trailing through various websites trying to find some information that could support him with these points. This is what excited me most about writing a book. In those few hours I had thought about nothing else but trying to find this information. My mind was free of other thoughts except for finding that information. This is what I needed in my life, something that would take my mind away from everything else and give me a focus outside of my life and work.

Two years ago I lost my best friend and hero, my dad. Since then, I have battled daily with what started as grief before being diagnosed with depression. Every day is a battle with my own brain and when left to think about things too much, can feel like a losing battle. The book in many ways has been a saviour for me. A way of getting away from these dark thoughts and low moods, just taking my mind to a different place. Depression is one of the most prevalent mental health disorders, affecting around 1 in 6 adults in the UK. The rates are also significantly higher than prior to the pandemic, with around 17% of adults in the UK having some form of depression, compared to 10% before the pandemic.

Approximately 280 million people in the world have depression. For a long time after his death, I expected to just feel better, and that the grief would subside like people told me it would. I had dealt with loss before, but nothing compared to how I felt every day. The worst thing about it is only those closest to me could see the pain I was in and often people who suffer depression will do so in silence. Work is a distraction and there I found it easy to hide, but at home it would be clear to see and would also effect those around me.

It was at this point that I first decided to seek help. Luckily for me I accessed support from the fantastic Sean's Place. This is a service open to men in Liverpool, who like me, suffer from various mental health conditions. Without them I don't know where I would be. That is another motivation for this book, to raise awareness for services like this, but also raise money for me to give back to them. I can never repay them for their help, but I hope this book can support them in some way with what they do. It's important to note that only 9% of men suffering from depression seek treatment, this was something I struggled with myself. If this book makes one person seek help, then this book will be a success.

Depression can lead to suicidal thoughts, I'm not ashamed to admit that the thought crosses my mind often. Would it take the pain away? No. It is permanent, an act which would cause more suffering for the ones I love. Due to their love for me and understanding my depression more myself, it is nothing more than a thought. In 2021, 5219 suicides were registered in the UK. This was 307 more than in 2020. This is a rate of 10.5 people per 100,000 in 2020, compared to 10.0 per 100,000 in 2019. The male suicide rate was 15.8 per 100,000, compared to a female suicide rate of 5.5 per 100,000. Around three-quarters of suicides were males (4,129 deaths; 74.0%) which is a truly shocking statistic. Again, if this book means somebody, just one person who has these thoughts seeks support or faces up to their issues, then again, I've achieved more than any sales of this book can generate financially.

Mental health isn't just limited to 'normal' people in society but also so-called celebrities. There have many deaths of high-profile figures caused by suicide and it shows fame and money cannot cover up the issues people face in their lives. The PFA did a study of footballers in the Premier League (PL) and the other English Football Leagues (EFL) in 2021-22. The data was gathered at wellbeing workshops held at clubs by the PFA during the 2021-22 season. It found 189 of the players - more than one-fifth - had experienced severe anxiety. "It could be peer-on-peer bullying, for example, from team-mates in the dressing room or training ground," Dr Michael Bennett, PFA Director of Wellbeing said on the bullying figures. "It could be by club staff or management. We are particularly concerned around transfer windows. We know that players can be isolated from their squads when a club is trying to force a move. We are often dealing with cases like this. Ultimately, whether it is the training ground or the stadium on a matchday, it's a player's workplace. They have a right to feel protected and safe at work. It feels obvious to state, but any form of bullying will have a lasting impact on an individual's mental health." Seventy-nine out of 843 male players in the Premier League and EFL surveyed across the course of last season said they had been bullied at some point in their professional life. Forty said they had experienced thoughts about taking their own life in the three months prior to completing the survey. Meaning almost 5% had suicidal thoughts. The data highlights the social and mental health challenges players face. "These are stark figures that illustrate how serious these issues are in the game," said Dr Bennett. The example of Gary Speed shows that football is not immune to the problems of suicide.

Although Speed is probably the one that first pops to mind when talking about footballers who have committed suicide, one that has stuck with me more is German national goalkeeper Robert Enke. Not much has been written about the reasons for why Speed killed himself. Whilst football and the pressures placed on professional footballers, was one of, if not the main cause for Enke's suicide.

Enke's issues with depression and how it affected his life is brilliantly told in the book, 'A Life Too Short: The Tragedy of Robert Enke' by his long-time friend and journalist Ronald Reng. It is one of the best sports books I've read and truly delves into the issues even our idols face. The idols we adore and that we watch on TV every week or in front of us live in a stadium, mental health affects us all, it doesn't discriminate.

Enke was a Germany international and had played for Mönchengladbach, Benfica and FC Barcelona (was loaned to Fenerbahçe and Tenerife during this spell), before signing for Hannover 96 in 2004. Enke's time in Barcelona almost certainly triggered the episodes of depression which ultimately led to his taking his life in November 2009. He managed to resurrect his career to the point where he was expected to be Germany's first choice goalkeeper at the 2010 World Cup. But the out-the-blue visits of paralytic fear and numbness never stopped chasing him and they returned with a vengeance during that autumn: on November 10th, two days after playing his 164th match for Hannover 96, he stepped in front of a Tuesday evening commuter train on its way from Bremen. He was 32 and left behind his wife, Teresa and Laila, their adopted daughter.

Barcelona pride themselves on being *"Més que un club"* (*"More than a club"*). The phrase was coined from a speech by former Club President Narcis de Carreras, who said in January 1968," Barcelona is something more than a football club. It is a spirit that is deep inside us, colours that we love above all else." Most football fans can agree that the colours of their club like Carreras talk about and the spirit deep inside us, make the club we support and love, more than just a club. This love for our club can cause fans to show their anger when things aren't going the way we want them. The same can be said for the media, who will highlight individual and team errors that have cost the team.

The pressure players face cannot be conceived by someone in the crowd, unless they themselves have played in front of thousands, with communities outside of the ground also focussing on a weekly football match like a religion. The argument is that they're paid enough, they should be able to deal with it. But no amount of money can keep the brain from being affected by negativity, especially when aimed directly at an individual. This is what Enke faced in his time at Barca, individual mistakes cost the team and this in turn led to him being ridiculed by fans and the media, with no support from inside the club either. With them more focussed on winning at all costs, than the individuals they have duty of care over. In the book Reng recalls a note that was found in Enke's hotel in Istanbul, during his loan spell at Fenerbache, in 2003:

"My year in Barcelona has changed me a lot. All the self-confidence that I built up in three years in Lisbon has been taken away from me…I was always glad I didn't have to play even in training games….. in reality I was always relaxed and happy when I was watching from the side-lines. I'm also really scared of the opinion of the public, the press and people's eyes. I'm paralysed by fear."

Just six years later this same fear resurfaced and truly didn't leave Enke. Losing his battle with depression, even when to others life seemed like it couldn't be better. The pressure of playing for a club such as Barca, or any team at the top level can be difficult for even anyone. To highlight this, you only have to look at even the most successful players. Even one of the most successful players in Barca's history, Andres Iniesta said this when he left to play in Japan. "Playing for Barca isn't just playing a football match. It's a brutal pressure, constant tension, training perfectly every day, being the best in every match." It was hard he concluded, "to enjoy it 100 percent."

A fact scarier than any other in the UK and should hopeful trigger anyone with dark thoughts to seek help is:
Suicide is the biggest killer in men under 50.

Football>Anything was chosen as the name for this book. For those unaware of the mathematical symbol >, this means greater than/more than. As a schoolteacher and head of maths it was important to try get some maths in. For myself Football is greater/more important than anything else in life (bar family/friends of course- just for those of you who have decided to read this book). This view is shared by many people across the world. In FIFA's latest estimates of fans worldwide, that 3.5 billion people consider themselves football fans. Of them 3.5 billion people, a staggering 265 million men and women play football worldwide. This puts football clearly at the top of most popular sports worldwide by estimate. It is followed by cricket, which has 2.5 billion fans and in third Field Hockey with 2 billion. These numbers are expected to continue to rise in football as popularity increases and through influencing new regions each year.

Football plays a huge part in society too. The Football Fandom in 2021 report found that 63 percent of people thought football helped them to develop a better understanding of social and economic issues through their love of football. Dr Martha Newson, Future Leaders Fellow at the University said this in relation to the report. "Football is now more representative than ever of the British public. Football is more than what happens on the pitch, it is entrenched in our day-to-day beliefs, embedded in our conversations, and shaping society and community behaviours". In my role as a Primary School Teacher, I have used football to motivate reluctant learners. Using their interest in football to engage them in learning, through themed activities or specific texts. Team sports in general have been a great way to show children different values in action and promote this to children with role models they see on TV or the internet.

Football is watched by huge numbers of people in the UK each year. Statista show that 32.46million people in the UK attended football matches in England's top four divisions in 2022. That shows 48% of the UK population attended football matches live in 2021/2022. 15 million of that aggregate score attended Premier League fixtures in 2021/2022. This jumps to 26.8 million people when you factor in TV coverage too. All this just shows to highlight how big football is and how things that take place in football are seen/discussed by people in the UK and Worldwide.

I was recently sat in Paris Beauvais airport, some 90km outside Paris city centre. It was 8.30 am on a Sunday morning and my flight home had been delayed for 3 hours. In the previous 48 hours, I'd had a grand total of 4 hours. That after flying from Oslo to Paris the morning before with a 3.30am wake up. After landing in Oslo at 10.30pm from Manchester, after a day teaching 32 Year 6 children. The reason for this ridiculous amount of travel was football. I had attended the Champions League final the night before. The game itself was awful from my perspective as a Liverpool fan. But the scenes outside the ground were horrendous. The treatment of Liverpool fans that night was shocking and the bone-chilling similarities to Hillsborough in 1989, where 97 Liverpool fans lost their lives was not lost on me. Fortunately, that night nobody died, but the lasting impact this will have on fans mentally is still to be seen. As well as the physical injuries and loss of personal belongings for some. The whole experience drained me emotionally, reading and hearing other people's experiences, when I had come away relatively unscathed.

This book isn't about Liverpool FC or will it detail events from the Paris Champions League Final 2022 again. But it is important for the book. Moments like that, make you question whether it was all worth it? The money spent by fans will have ranged into the multiple thousands. I know many who had to pay £2000 for tickets alone. But more importantly was it worth it from an experience point of view. Football is a sport that takes you on an emotional rollercoaster and gives you experiences no other sport can. But although football doesn't always give you highs and depending on the team you support it could be frequent lows. The love of football, the love of the team you follow, creates a bond that cannot be broken. Some of you reading now may be thinking, wow he's complaining about going to a Champions League final. I'm not, obviously I wish it was a different result, but that's football. The answer to the question above. Was it all worth it? Yes, and I'd do it again tomorrow. Why? Because I love football and my team so much.

My love of football wasn't started watching the premier league though. My love for football grew from grassroots, a shared love that was created through an extremely close bond with my dad. This would see me watching my dad play in local amateur football leagues on Sundays from an early age. Watching him play 5-a-side every Thursday night as I played in empty goals at the side of the pitch. But most importantly for me being able to see up close and personal the background of football from inside a dressing room. My dad was a physio for various non-league clubs around Merseyside and it was here that I learnt so much about football. More than you could ever learn watching an interactive pitch with arrows appear on it on the TV (not knocking this BTW, I love MNF). It taught me so much as a person in terms of social interaction and hard work (filling water bottles and ice boxes weren't easy for a 6-year-old). It helped me to develop as a footballer, seeing tactics and football that close. It was here that I developed my love for football. I was in awe of the players; they were heroes to me. More so than a Liverpool player at the time. Why? Because I could relate and interact with these people. I could see how genuine they were and how much they loved football. I sat on the bench with the players and my dad.

(Sometimes hidden if a linesman was being particularly busy) It showed me the raw emotion of football in celebration but also despair.

Football has been something that has brought me so much joy and despair through my life. It is like a drug to me and many others, but after my dad's death, I struggled to even find solace in my passion. The moment that changed that was around 3 months after his death when Liverpool goalkeeper Alisson Becker, scored a last-minute winner for Liverpool against West Brom. Not because Liverpool had won, but the person who had done it. Alisson himself had lost his father recently too. The emotional release from him, released from me too, I found myself crying with him. After the game Alisson told Sky Sports this: "Football is my life...I hope my father was there to see it with God on his side celebrating. I have been away from interviews for a long time because it was difficult - I always get emotional on that subject. But I want to thank all of you, all the Premier League, all the players and teams, I've had letters, for example, from Everton, Man City, Chelsea [and more]. I want to say thank you. If it wasn't for you all I could never have got through it."

That moment made me realise that football can get you through the dark times. That joy and adulation it gives you cannot be compared to, even though it isn't always that way. That moment brought back all the memories I shared with my dad through football, whether it be going to the match together or him teaching me how to play from an early age. Alisson had shown strength that I couldn't up to that point, although he was struggling personally, that moment was a relief for him to. It's not always that easy though. Another Brazilian who was a cult figure in football in the 2000s and had the world at his feet was the striker Adriano. He was one of the best strikers in the world at one point and was unstoppable to defenders, playing for Inter Milan and Brazil. However, that suddenly stopped, and his peak reached an untimely end. He disappeared into obscurity as he returned to Brazil and played there with a few loan spells back in Europe. The reason this happened. His father died just like Alisson. "So, when my father died, football was never the same. I was across the ocean in Italy, away from my family, and I just couldn't cope with it. I got so depressed, man. I started drinking a lot... It had nothing to do with Inter. I just wanted to go home," Adriano said years later. Who knows what he could've went on to do, but for a few years he was the most feared player in world football, powering Brazil to Copa America titles and Confederation cups, the heir apparent to Ronaldo. He is now back in the favelas where he grew up and was cleared of drug trafficking charges in 2014, due to lack of evidence.

Although the experiences of being my dad's shadow as a child, taught me so many valuable things in terms of playing and understanding football. As well as developing my social outlook on life. It also opened my eyes from a young age to the dark side of football. This is what this book will focus on, along with the effect this has on the mental health of all those involved. It will not share my experiences from a non-league perspective. But examples from some of the biggest stars and clubs in word football. The similarities are closer than you would ever think, considering we are comparing small community clubs and worldwide brands.

What I learnt quickly is that you must win at all costs. Football is a ruthless sport and never more so than at that level. Lots of players are on non-contract terms, meaning one bad result and you will be back playing with your mates the week after. In a study by Statista, it showed 25% of players and managers in non-league football believed they had mental health issues. This rises to 38% when looking at those aged 26-29. This was affected by the suspension of play due to COVID but shows the pressure players are under to play. The same applies to managers though, the turnover in mangers is extremely high. If a manager is released, it means his backroom staff will leave with him too (Coaches and Physio). It's not rare to see multiple managers in a season at Step 3 below (Northern/Southern Premier league). Often it can be before the season even starts. The book will look at winning at all costs from a professional standpoint. With the chapters in this section looking at: Murder, Performance Enhancing Drugs, Recreational Drugs, Match-Fixing and Injuries.

As far as I am aware Murder and Match-Fixing are both things I didn't witness as a child when I was around non-league teams. However, all the other things are things I was aware of as a child. Injuries were an obvious thing I saw as my dad was the Physio and he had to deal with the players injuries. This would often see his thoughts be overlooked by managers as they sought to play their strongest team despite the affects this could have on players. Players themselves would make this decision, as often they were only paid if they played; meaning if they could move, even limited, then they would try and be on the pitch at some point in the game. Non-league football isn't professional football, and the drinking culture hasn't really eradicated itself like it has in the professional game. Away buses home would be a big piss up if the result had gone the right way. Players wouldn't take drugs on the coach but just like others in society would do in their social lives. An estimated 1 in 11 adults aged 16 to 59 years had taken a drug in 2022-2023 (9.4%; approximately 3.2 million people). When you change this to the demographic of what most footballers in the team were, around one in five adults aged 16 to 24 years had taken a drug in the last year (21%; approximately 1.3 million people).

Sometimes players would turn up from being out the night before (which most of us have at points) but this has happened in professional football too. A few players I remember as being what I'd describe as a 'juice head' or scientifically know as a user of performance enhancing drugs (PEDs). This wasn't taken to make them the best player on the pitch, but more out of vanity and wanting to look good. This wouldn't be stopped in non-league football as there is no testing of players as the cost is too much for leagues below the conference, so players are free to do what they want. However, in professional football this comes with a huge price for those caught taking them. Non-league football taught me that to win you will do anything, most of the time from cheating; through foul means on the pitch or antics to distract others off it.

The other thing that my experiences as a child taught me and which has stuck with me more than others is football is run by those powered by greed. The most successful non-league teams have the best team. In some cases, this may be due to just getting a group together who gel and know how to win, but more often and not success is powered by money. Having the biggest budget gets you the best team. Teams like Crawley, Fleetwood and Forest Green bought their way through the leagues. At times you've got teams paying an individual player more than their whole budget for 15 players. If things aren't going, we'll teams can have their budgets taken away too. I've witnessed players not being paid due to bad performances by chairmen and how management teams are treated when things don't go well.

The second half of the book looks at Greed. The chapters look at: Gambling, Ownership and Governance. Ownership in non-league for most is a thankless task. It will see lots pump money into a team they have some ties to or local area, with not much return. In some rare cases though a team may have huge attendances for the level and if they own the rights to the ground and the bar, see some make lots of money. In turn this should be reinvested and see the team improve with the attendance. A good source of local pride in the community is what entices people to avoid the big boys and attend and some teams in my local area have done a great job of this. What my local area has not had is a millionaire/ss who will use a club as a real-life version of football manager. They pump money into these clubs and climb the ladders before reaching a ceiling, where their money doesn't match that of the owners in the league they reach. Like what happened with the above-mentioned teams before, who can gazump the wage bills of non-league teams but then not do the same in the EFL.

The book will look at billionaires instead of millionaires and how this has changed the state of football. Gambling like recreational drugs is an issue in society and not just solely linked to football or footballers. However, there were teams my dad was involved with where gambling came under the spotlight when players were caught betting on the outcome of their own teams' games. In most cases even for their own team and still being punished. The same would happen with inside information you aren't privy to at the top level, with friends talking between themselves and discussing injuries and this informing whether a team was weakened enough to then add the other team to your accumulator. Governance in this book will cover all aspects from local to national to global but if you've been involved in football in any form then you will have an opinion of your local FA or council. Football has been underfunded for a long time and this reflected in the state of the facilities we played on as children. As we've grown older the cost of playing on these already poor facilities has continued to rise and football is no longer a cheap hobby to keep. From 5-a-side prices to subs, it prices out some youngsters and demographics from playing anything other than an unorganised kick about.

Writing this book though and understanding my own battle with my mental health, what has struck me especially looking at the shocking statistics associated with suicide in the UK is this.

LIFE>ANYTHING

Something that in my darkest days I need to remind myself, even though that seems tough and not the answer, when you feel like you're losing the battle against the dark thoughts in your head. Life>Anything, goes away from the Shankly quote at the beginning of the chapter, about football being more important than life and death. For a large portion of my life, I felt football was the most important thing in my life. But after losing my dad and hitting rock bottom, my saviour is the birth of my two little boys. Without them I don't know whether I would have the strength to go on, but they have showed me more than anything that Life>Anything.

PART I

WIN AT ALL COSTS

1

Murder

"Life doesn't end here. We must go on. Life cannot end here. No matter how difficult, we must stand back up."
Andrés Escobar

After Colombia's elimination from USA 1994, Escobar penned the

following words for Bogota's El Tiempe newspaper:

The 23rd June 1994, a day when the hosts of the 1994 World Cup secured their first victory of the tournament, in front of their own jubilant supporters. That day the USA beat Colombia, one of the teams mooted to win the whole tournament. The 2-1 victory would play a pivotal role in allowing them to qualify for the knockout stages of the tournament. This following an opening fixture draw against Switzerland, before defeat to Romania, who had defeated Colombia by 3-1 in the opening fixture. The 4 points were enough to qualify the US as one of the four best third-placed sides.

This gave the US men's team a dream fixture against the eventual champions Brazil. Although this last 16 tie resulted in defeat, this was their best finish at a World Cup since 1930, only bettered once after in 2002 (reached QF). The team won over the US public, one that had been very sceptical of not only the team but the sport in general. This would change the direction of 'Soccer' for generations to come, all caused by the national team's success at the tournament. Therefore, you would be led to believe that the win over Colombia that day would be most remembered for the transformation it caused to US soccer. Bur, that's not the case, an incident in the 34th minute of the game, would send shockwaves around the world.

The moment in the 34th minute of the match is one that any defender has come face to face with. Whether you are a Sunday league defender or an experienced international defender. It is a situation that you dread, a low driven cross across the box. Opposition striker behind you. The ball in no-man's land for the goalkeeper. Your positioning means you can only stretch to attempt to clear it, a clear connection isn't guaranteed. The two options the defender has are: 1. Leave the ball in the hope the striker misjudges his run/finish 2. Stretch for the ball and hope the contact is good enough to clear the ball for a corner. The option any sane defender takes in that situation is option 2. That day the cross came from US midfielder John Harkes. The striker in the box was Earnie Steward. The defender Andrés Escobar. Escobar did choose option 2, his lunge to stop the ball reaching Steward, instead deflected the ball into his own goal. The inexperienced 22-year-old Colombian goalkeeper Oscar Cordoba didn't move as the ball passed him into the back of the net. This was one of the four goals Colombia conceded at the 1994 World Cup, two coming in the game against the US. However, no goal in the history of football may have had the ramifications that fateful own goal would have.

Colombia is a country in South America with an insular region in North America. It is the only country in South America with coastlines and islands along both the Atlantic and Pacific Oceans. Over the last decade Colombia has experienced a historic economic boom. Poverty has decreased by an average of 1.35% per year since 1990, dropping from 65% in 1990 to 27% by 2018. With the third-largest diversified economy in South America.

However, Colombia's international image was in tatters in the 1980s. The Colombian government's relationship with drug cartels and reluctance to punish cartel leaders, had caused tensions with the US government. The leader of the Medellin Cartel, the second biggest city in Colombia, is probably the most infamous drug lord of all-time. Pablo Emilio Escobar Gavira, commonly known as Pablo Escobar. Although Pablo and Andrés shared the same surname, they were of no relation. Their lives would intertwine, but similarities in both men, were few and far between.

At its peak the cartel supplied 80% of America's cocaine, making Pablo at the time the seventh richest person in the world. To put into context how much money the Medellin cartel was making in tax-free profit every year between 1981-86, we can compare the profits in this period to one of the UK's richest organisations BP in 2021. According to Forbes, the Medellin cartel were making annually $7 billion. BP in 2021 reported profits of $7.55 billion, showing the size of the operation Escobar had created.

Escobar and other cartel leaders saw an opportunity in Colombian domestic football. When your earnings are illicit, you need to find a way to clear this money through legal holding companies. Football was the answer. Cartel leaders bought football teams in their region, pumping their drug money into the clubs and in doing so laundering their money. This period of football in Colombia was known as 'Narco Soccer'.

Although, this partnership would have serious consequences for lots of aspects of football in Colombia. This money allowed the Colombian Primera league to thrive and in doing so led to a golden era for the Colombian National team. The club chosen by Pablo to bankroll was Atlético Nacional, a team in Medellin. He was however never appointed as an owner or director but was the ultimate decision maker at the club. His rivals in the Cali cartel (Orejuela brothers) bankrolled América de Cali, whilst his ally and friend Jose Gacha bought Millionarios, at the time the most famous club in Colombia.

Pablo Escobar will divide opinion of everyone around the world but even more so in his own country. He has a near-mythic legacy, that displays how wildly schizophrenic his character is. One side of his character is his dark side, he was a brutal terrorist who ordered killings, coordinated kidnappings and bullied his way to the top, overseeing an unscrupulous dynasty of rampant corruption. On the other hand, though, he is cast as the modern-day Robin Hood, robbing from the rich and giving to the poor in a selfless crusade to redress the chronic inequalities of Colombian life.

How he is seen in Colombia is dependent on the class of the person. Angel or devil? Hero or villain? Saviour or tormentor? Even those who were meant to be against him, law enforcement, state officials or high-ranking government officials, were under his control, while any who showed opposition would be removed or assassinated. He committed terrorist attacks against his own country and killed political candidates, who didn't fit his agenda. It is estimated by some that 5,000 people were murdered by his henchmen. But although his regime ruined the lives of so many, he also changed the lives of others for the good. He built housing developments in the poorest areas of Medellín, who had been forgotten by the government. He transformed rubbish dumps into acceptable accommodation for the neediest in society, providing schools, medical centres and much-needed greenery that enriched countless lives. He donated to worthy causes and inspired the poorest people in Colombian society to aspire to do more with their lives and see outside of their barrios. The debate will rage on forever, whether he was good or bad, but he did both and that's what makes him so polarising.

His outlet to remove himself from all the carnage that followed him in his life and his passion outside of making money was football. The 'beautiful game' was his drug, like so many of us too. He was loco for football, and it played a huge role in his personal and professional development. His passion for the sport saw him use his power and money to bring about positive changes to the sport in his country. He built football pitches for local communities, donated floodlights and equipment that would allow locals to play whenever they wanted. A little like we have seen in our country now and with football, entering competitions and joining teams was expensive, but Escobar *democratised* football in his homeland, financing the infrastructure it needed to blossom. He organised tournaments in the barrios and would be there as a spectator, before addressing the crowds with passionate speeches. He was a hero to those who came to watch, large crowds would gather to watch these amateur showcases and he would be swarmed, signing autographs and speaking to those in attendance.

Like football has done for many, he gave people the chance to escape their lives through football and used this to continue to create his persona to the poorer parts of Colombian society. Like many notable players in history who started playing football on the streets, the first chance some talents got was through the help of Pablo. Future Colombian internationals such as Alexis García, Chico Serna and Pacho Maturana rose from the Medellín slums to carve out professional careers, honing their skills on Pablo's pitches. The most notable though of all these to come from the slums was René Higuita, who we will discuss in this chapter.

Like everything else in his life though, the food was also followed by the bad. Football was being used as an unlikely pawn in the quest for one-upmanship. Football was useful in many ways for Cartel kingpins. The game had unregulated finances, and this allowed the Cartels to take advantage. They used the support of loyal fans, to improve their image to the public, legitimising these criminal businessman as local heroes, who funded the dreams of so many and developing communities. For many, like everything else in society that the drugs trade had got its claws into, it was inevitable that football would also become embroiled. Unfortunately, this came true and Colombian gangsters turned football into a microcosm of their territorial battles over narcotics.

Football became anything but the 'beautiful game'. Referees were attacked, hooliganism in the stands took over and bribes were commonplace, ruining the integrity of the competition in the country. The league became a farce, as professional football was taken over by the rich and morally bankrupt, whose corruption made the entire league a farce. Those who contested this ownership, were removed like anyone else in society, who contested their control. This was the fate of Rodrigo Bonilla, who was a leading figure in the campaign to end cartel ownership of Colombian football clubs. He found himself assassinated on the orders of Escobar, who felt that Bonilla had a perceived bias against the Medellín cartel. As he continued to create problems for the government and its officials, football was seen as the lesser of many evils, apparently, and the kingpins ran amok.

It is said that the idea of Pablo taking over football clubs was floated by his brother Roberto. He oversaw the cartel' accounts and he understood that they needed to constantly look for outlets for the huge amount of wealth his brother had. Football due to its unregulated finances seemed to be a viable option and is when the drugs empire began funnelling money into Nacional, allowing the club to purchase, develop and retain the best players from across

Colombia. Surprisingly though, he didn't forget about their less successful city rivals DIM, occasionally helping his boyhood club through times of distress. Under Pablo's control, the Nacional wage bill grew to millions of dollars per year, a sheer abnormality in Colombian society. Players also received huge bonuses for winning key matches, sometimes extending to $8,000, more than many Colombians made *in an entire year*. Naturally, top stars wanted to play for Escobar amid such gross generosity, and many were willing to ignore his reputation outside of football to maximise their earnings during a relatively short playing career.

The crowds at the clubs were used to launder their dirty money. All tickets were sold in cash at turnstiles, which allowed the bosses to lie about attendance figures and wash their dirty money. Nacional's stadium held around 40,000 fans, yet even though there were clear spaces in the crowd, most games were reported as sell-outs. The technique would also be used with merchandising, with sales figures and concessions sales being doctored. This made Colombian football clubs appear far more lucrative than they ever were. Transfers were another way they were able to launder their money. The drug lords would swap players for crazy and fictional fees. For example, if a club sold a player for $1 million, it was easy to report that officially as, say, $3 million, legitimising dark money in the cartel accounts. This was a daily occurrence as likeminded kingpins colluded together to support each other to legitimise their money. The last way they were able to obtain money from football was through football betting. Club owners would back their own teams in matches, wagering millions of dollars on disputed games. The vast sums of money were ploughed into authorised bookmakers, making the match-fixing rumours even more prevalent. Through this betting, it was relatively easy to transform, say, $50,000 of filthy money into $250,000 of *laundered* money. Escobar even created his own version of fantasy football or Ultimate team. He would pick and pay professional players from a range of top clubs to compete in matches at Hacienda Nápoles, his luxurious estate. Foreign players were even flown in for those games, which typically pitted Pablo against his associates, with bets on the outcome of such exhibitions often surpassing $2 million. When gambles failed though and the agreed to outcome wasn't meant, like whenever else they were not pleased, the cartel would seek retribution. In 1989, for example, referee Alvaro Ortega was gunned down after disallowing an important goal in a game between DIM and América de Cali. The drug bosses were said to be furious at the decision, which cost them a small fortune in dodgy bets, and Ortega paid with his life, a stark reminder of just how evil these people were.

The money that was pumped into football was the ironic legacy that would see the rise of the Colombian national football team. Even though the money was dirty, it meant better facilities, bigger wages, improved training techniques and greater retention of talent. The generous contracts prevented the top players leaving, improving the overall standard of play in the country. The legacy can still be seen in Colombian football, with starts plying their trade all over the world, with some of the biggest stars such as Luis Diaz and Davidson Sanchez both playing in the Premier League. The legacy can still be seen at grassroots though, with football still being played on the fields Escobar built, although the name has changed, and they have been renovated. Stars are still honed on those pitches and the legacy, even if shrouded by a dark cloud, is a positive for those even at the bottom rung of society in Colombia.

How this all links to Andrés is that at the age of 19 he was signed by his future Colombia national team manager Francisco

Maturana to play for Atlético. Andrés was born in Calasanz, Medellin on 13th March 1967. Unlike many of his teammates, who grew up in poor neighbourhoods, with pitches funded by the cartel, Andrés grew up in a middle-class family. This may show why later in life Andrés shunned the lavish parties thrown by Pablo and didn't share the same sense of loyalty as others around him. His father Dario was a banker, and the family grew up devout Catholics, with Andrés attending church each morning before school. From a young age Andrés stood out as an outstanding player but still excelled at school, before being supported by his family to turn professional. His sister Maria Ester talked about how Andrés' mother's death at the age of 52 also influenced his decision. She said in an interview with ESPN, "Mum passed away at 52 with cancer. It was especially difficult for Andrés, but football allowed him to channel his feeling and his pain". Playing alongside him at Atlético was his brother Santiago.

Andrés was a defender throughout his career and wore the number 2. His nickname was 'El Caballero del Fútbol', which translates to 'The Gentleman of Football'. 2 years after making his debut for Atlético, Andrés received his first call up for the Colombian national team. He made his debut against Canada in a 3-0 win on 30th March 1988. This was then followed by his appearances in the 1988 Rous cup, a tournament between Scotland, England and Colombia. This was the fourth staging of the competition, based around the England-Scotland rivalry. The previous year had seen Brazil invited, but this time the South American opposition for the two home nations would be Colombia. In their first game, Colombia drew 0-0 with Scotland at Hampden Park. The second game of the cup Colombia played England at Wembley, needing a win to lift the cup. England took the lead through the former Everton and at the time Barcelona striker Gary Lineker. In the 66th minute Andrés rose highest at a corner to score his first and what would be last goal for the national team, resulting in a 1-1 draw with England and a second placed finish. His brother Santiago in an interview with the Daily Mirror before England played Colombia at the 2018 World Cup described it as, "The highest and happiest moment of his life." His sister Maria Ester agreed, "That goal against England brought Andrés so much happiness, something he carried with him for all his life, because it was his first and only international goal for Colombia. It was the highest and happiest moment of his life". To highlight the strength of his club side Atlético, 7 of the starting 11 for the Colombian national team belonged to Atlético. This side managed to match stride for stride an England team including: Lineker, Barnes, Robson and Hoddle to name a few. Whilst Scotland couldn't boast as many star names, they were no mugs, qualifying in 1990 for their fifth consecutive world cup, finishing second in qualifying behind only France.

Whilst 1988 was a hugely successful year for Andrés personally making his national team debut, as a club 1989 would be the best in the history of Atlético. This would also go down as the most successful season had by a Colombian team up to that point. 1989 saw the Pablo Escobar bankrolled Atlético win the Copa Libertadores. In doing so they became the first Colombian team to win South America's marquee club tournament (equivalent of the European cup). To show the magnitude of this the club had only existed for 42 years, after being founded in 1947. To compare this to English football the team to be formed closest to the formation of Atlético was Burton Albion in 1950. Their biggest achievement to date is League one runners up. In European football, the equivalent is VfL Wolfsburg in the German Bundesliga, who were formed in 1945. Although they have won the Bundesliga and German cup, their best finish in the Champions league was reaching the quarter finals in 2015-16.

Andrés was the main stay of the defence and the standout player of the team. However, he was supported by a cast of recognisable names such as his national teammate, goalkeeper René Higuita otherwise known as "El Loco" for his risky style of play. A goalkeeper who epitomised the now commonly known term of "sweeper keeper", used to describe goalkeepers such as Manuel Neuer etc. Higuita was pioneering in his influence for how goalkeepers were viewed and positional further from the goal. Higuita's extravagant style of play however could at times not come off with dire consequences and 'El Loco' wasn't just a madman on the pitch, but also off it. The other most recognisable name in the squad and a national teammate was Faustino Asprilla. The forward who would go on to play for Parma in Serie A and the Newcastle in the Premier League. On a personal level Asprilla's richest vein of form was only bettered in his time at Parma, were in 1993 he scored 4 goals in 8 games, as they lifted the European Cup Winners Cup. Much like Atlético, this helped Parma to win their first ever international tournament. This was quickly followed by a 2-1 defeat (over 2 legs) of AC Milan the European champions, who boasted the formidable defensive partnership of Franco Baresi and Paolo Maldini.

On their way to the title, Atlético played their domestic rivals Millionaris in an all-Colombian quarter final. This pitted two of the Narco backed teams against each other as Pablo's Atlético played his ally in the drug trade Jose Gacha's backed Millionaris. It's important to note the magnitude of this. The Copa Liberatedores was the pinnacle of club football in South America and here we had two teams bankrolled by drug money playing in the quarter final of that tournament. The equivalent of an all-English tie in the quarter finals of the Champions League, but rather than the teams being financed by foreign owners. The club has been financed by millions of pounds from local drug dealers who bankroll the clubs. Imagine Curtis Warren funding Liverpool's progress to a Champions League quarter final, it's just unheard of anywhere else in the world. The two-legged tie between the two Colombian sides was not shy of controversy though. Atlético won 2-1 over both legs, but Millionaris were denied a penalty to level the tie, when 'El Loco' mistimed a slide tackle and giving a clear penalty. However, the appeals for the penalty were waved away, much to the relief of Higuita. Rumours have swirled ever since of Cartel involvement and bribing of the referee and officials, which has never been proven, despite the evidence pointing to a penalty.

The semi-finals however were much more straightforward as Atlético defeated Uruguay's Danubio 6-0 over two legs. Unlike the European equivalent of a one-off final, the Copa Liberatadores is played over two legs. The opposition in the final was Paraguay's Olimpia, who had won the tournament previously in 1979 and would go on to win it the following year too. Olimpia was led by the tournament's top goal scorer and former FC Barcelona forward Raul Vicente Amarilla (10 goals). It was fortunate for Atlético that the game was over two legs, as the first leg ended disastrously in a 2-0 defeat. Fortunately for Atlético the first leg had taken place in Paraguay, in front of 50,000 Olimpia fans. In the return leg, Atlético would be cheered on by up to 60,000 fans. The match had been moved from Medeliin and Atlético's stadium to the countries capital Bogota and the Estadio El Campin. This shows the magnitude of the game not only for Atlético but also for Colombia itself, as their home ground was deemed too small for a tie of this size. Cheered on by a sea of green and white, Atlético were able to turn around the tie and win 2-0, with two second half goals. After a tense period of extra-time the game went to penalties. Olimpia would've been seen as favourites to win this penalty shootout as twice on their way to the final, they had won on penalties. Firstly, defeating Argentine giants Boca Juniors in the last 16, before then defeating Brazil's Internacional in the semi-finals. Andrés stepped up and took the first penalty scoring for Atlético. Just like his general style of play stepping up and taking the first penalty, scoring a pressure penalty, showed the calmness Andrés displayed on the pitch. Both teams would eventually take 9 penalties each. Higuita was performing heroics in goal saving 5 penalties, whilst also scoring his own penalty. Scoring goals for goalkeepers can be quite a rare commodity, but Higuita was renowned for it. He scored 41 goals in his career, ranking him in the top ten highest goal scoring goalkeepers of all time. Whilst Higuita was performing heroic in goal, his team were struggling to score their own penalties. Coming up to their final penalty the scores were level at 4-4, meaning they had missed four themselves. The responsibility fell to Andrés international teammate, midfielder Leonel Alvarez (need symbol above A). Fortunately, Alvarez kept his cool sending the keeper the wrong way with a stuttered run, making history as Atlético became the first Colombian team in history to lift the Copa Libertadores.

To celebrate this amazing feat the players were flew to Pablo's lavish ranch for a huge party to celebrate their success. Each player was given a cash bonus for their achievement, and it was said that Pablo also raffled off a brand-new truck that night to the players too. The whole team attended this party, but Andrés didn't feel comfortable in these surroundings and revealed his reservations to those closest to him. Whilst Andrés had his reservations, he understood where the money came from that he was being paid. However, he wanted to use this to better the lives of children in Medellin, one thing he did was fund scholarships in his old school for disadvantaged children. Pablo saw all the players as his friends and although not close to Andrés as some of the players from poorer backgrounds, admired him greatly.

The reward for winning the Copa Libertadores was the chance to win the 1989 Intercontinental cup against the best team in Europe. This has now been rebranded as the FIFA Club World Cup but has often been seen as the pinnacle for any South American team to win, by proving they're better than the European giants. The European giants they would be facing off against in Tokyo, Japan would be AC Milan and their ground-breaking manager Arrigo Sacchi. Sacchi is regarded by many as one of the greatest managers of all-time, whilst his Milan side from 1987-91 as one of the best teams in history. His team were built on outstanding defensive strength, with the quartet of Maldini, Baresi, Costacurta and Tassoti, anchoring a fluid 4-4-2 formation. Sacchi would take over as Italy manager in 1991 and was the man in charge of Italy at the 1994 World Cup, using the same quartet to reach the World Cup Final were they were beat on penalties by Brazil.

Sacchi's trusted scout Natale Bianchedi was sent to Colombia on a scouting mission to see what he could find out about their relatively unknown opponents. The trip however would be fruitless for Bianchedi and Sacchi, as when he arrived in Medellin, he was shocked to find that all Colombian football had been suspended by the government. The reason probably shocked him more, the assassination of referee Alvaro Ortega, reportedly on the orders of a disgruntled Pablo Escobar. Escobar was not happy with the refereeing performance of Ortega in a match Atlético had lost to his rival the Cali Cartel's funded America de Cali. The punishment for this was death in Escobar's eyes.

Therefore, Atlético came as a complete surprise package for Sacchi and his AC team. However, with the talent at his disposal it was Atlético who were worried. With the formidable defence supported by the Dutch attacking flair of Marco Van-Basten and Frank Rijkaard, with future AC Milan manger Carlo Ancelloti also playing in midfield. The game was played in the national stadium in Tokyo and was watched by 60,288 players. It was Milan who were renowned for their defending, but Andrés and his teammates showed their own credentials and defended heroically. After 90 minutes the game finished 0-0, with both teams continuing to cancel each other out. The game looked like it was destined for penalties and the chance for 'El Loco' to perform heroics again, until heartbreak in the 119th minute. Substitute Albergio Evani scored a curling free kick, to break the Colombian's hearts in what had been a valiant effort against the best team in Europe. This was proven once again the following year as AC won back-to-back European cups in 1990. Andrés however had left a lasting impression on AC Milan, as in the build-up to the World Cup 1994 he had been approached to sign that summer, for what the Italians thought would be a long-term replacement for Franco Baresi. Although, some thought these would be impossible shoes to fill, Andrés had decided this was a new challenge he would face with his fiancé Pamela Cascardo after the World Cup.

1994 would not be the first time that Andrés played in Europe though. He had a brief 8 game spell playing for BSC Young Boys in Switzerland for 8 games. Not much is known in terms of the reasons for this short-lived tenure. But looking at the dates, one would presume this was a short loan during the suspension of the Colombian League due to Ortega's death in 1989. The year before the US 94 World Cup saw Colombia have their best result at the Copa America 1993 as they finished 3rd place, defeating Argentina 2-1 (Won the Copa America in 2001). But it was another defeat of

Argentina, in World Cup Qualification that made the whole world stand up and take notice of this "Golden Generation' of Colombian football. Argentina needed to win to secure qualification, with a draw being good enough for Colombia. What happened in the game is still remembered by all Colombians to this day. The 3rd September 1993 is still celebrated annually by Colombians known as 'El Cinco-Cero'. The translation was a 5-0 victory, in Argentina, a team who hadn't lost at home in 6 years and had never in their history conceded five goals at home. Two goals apiece from the lively Freddy Rincon and Faustino Asprilla, with Adolfo Valencia rounding off the rout. Throughout the game, the creative playmaker Carlos Valderrama pulled the strings, regarded as the best Colombian player of all-time, he would be awarded the 1993 South American Player of the Year. World Soccer also named him one of the top 100 players of the 20th Century. In an interview with ESPN, Valderrama said this about that memorable night, "I knew we had made history. Nobody had ever beaten Argentina 5-0. We had qualified for the World Cup, but the most emotional thing was the Argentina fans giving us a standing ovation".

The game would have significant consequences for both teams. Colombia were now being tipped as favourites to win the whole World Cup, with Brazil legend Pele declaring them as a team he expected to reach at least the semi-finals of the tournament. This was supported by FIFA's ranking, who at the start of World Cup qualification had them placed 34th in the world, now ranked them 4th in the world. Football though had allowed Colombia to unite the country behind them, even in times of struggle. With Cartel related killings making Colombia the murder capital of the world. Qualifying for the World Cup in the USA of all places too allowed them the opportunity to change the perceived impression of all Colombian's formed due to the relationship with Pablo Escobar and the cartels. In response to their humbling defeat Argentina would turn to their enigmatic saviour Diego Maradona, in the hope he could galvanise the team at the World Cup and allow Argentina to better their second-place finish at the 1990 World Cup. However, this would end in disaster and be looked at in more detail in (Section of book to be added).

The years following Atlético 's Copa Libertadores win had not been as fortunate as the Colombian Football Teams fortunes for Pablo. In 1991, he surrendered to the Colombian Authorities on the promise he wouldn't be extradited to America. He was sentenced to five years jail and was imprisoned in his own self-made prison Le Catedral. This prison allowed Escobar to run his organisation as he had done on the outside. He owned the guards at the prison, and this allowed him to do as he please. This included allowing him to host football games with some of the world's best footballers, being flown in for Pablo's pleasure. The Colombian national team were also sent for and took part in a football match with Pablo joining in. Once again this deeply worried Andrés and he was very reluctant to visit the jail but like his sister Maria stated to ESPN, "He didn't have a choice. You had to go play or else".

1992 though saw the government be tired of Escobar and his 'self-made prison' and when they went to capture him to rehouse him in a government prison he escaped. Worse things were coming however though, he was now not just on the run from the government, but at war with 'Los Pepes'. Los Pepes (People persecuted by Escobar) was created by Pablo's rivals in the Cali Cartel and paramilitary leader Carlos Castano. With support from the government and attacks on those close to Escobar, Pablo was losing the war. The government with information from Los Pepes and Castano (once close to Pablo) found Pablo on 2nd December

1993. He was shot and killed trying to escape. After the effect he had on football in Colombia, he would not see the 'Golden Generation' on the biggest stage. Colombia manager Francisco Marturana realised the effect he had, "Two things allowed Colombian football to reach the levels it did. One we had a very good team, but two we had the money to pay the top players and keep them in the country. We didn't change anything we did, but the level of play went up". His death would create a vacuum for power in Medellin, the Colombia players left for the World Cup with a backdrop of lawlessness and death, as rival drug factions fought for power. This lawlessness would have dire consequences for Andrés too.

Colombia's preparations for the World Cup were far from perfect. Their 28-game unbeaten streak came to an end in a friendly with Bolivia in the build-up to the tournament. Worse was to come though, Rene Higuita would not be going to the tournament. He had been arrested and charged with Kidnapping. He would serve seven months in prison. Once again this connected to Pablo, who had asked 'El Loco' to retrieve ransom money from drug dealer Carlos Molina for the release of his daughter. This is illegal in Colombia, as the money he received from Pablo for acting as a go-between means he profited from a kidnapping. In the ESPN documentary 'The Two Escobars', Higuita denies this was the reason he was locked up though. "When they arrested me all they asked was questions about Pablo. Pablo gave so many of us players so many things. All I wanted to do was thank him for that. I didn't think this was illegal." The theory he was made an example of just for his relationship with Pablo and visiting him in prison was supported by many. Although he wouldn't be charged, Colombia didn't have their long-standing goalkeeper at the World Cup.

In Matthew Evans USA 94: The World Cup That Changed The Game, he speaks to Colombian football expert and British journalist Carl Worswick. Worswick talks about how the Colombian team had captured the hearts of the nation and had created some of the country's first iconic players. However, he also noted how nobody quite knew how to deal with the defeat of Argentina and things began to spiral out of control. Mirroring what was happening in Colombian society at the time with the death of Pablo. To create even more issues in the build-up to the tournament he talks about how the team became "the football world's Harlem Globetrotters", as they played some 30 warm-up games, with tours of the Middle East and US included in this.

It wasn't just the Colombian football federation who were cashing in on this newfound success though, players had also cashed in and according to Worswick, "Egos ballooned, business and political interests meddled with the side, and nobody was able to repress the monster that the result had given birth to". The preparations had been far from perfect for a team tipped to win the whole tournament and once again problems in Colombian society and Medellin would rear its ugly head again. Colombian defender Luis 'Chonto' Herrera's son was kidnapped in Medellin. His son was 2-years old and according to the player himself, was kidnapped by "local thugs". Fortunately, his son was returned safely, but the player himself highlighted how this wouldn't have happened if Pablo was still there. "With the boss not there anymore, everyone became their own boss". Andrés was also not immune to the war for power in Medellin. His fiancé Pamela Cascardo remembers a time when they were 5 minutes from potential death, when visiting a shopping plaza. 5 minutes before their arrival a huge bomb went off killing many innocent civilians. It was at this moment she says, "One learns to cherish each moment, we decided to marry and start a family". The issues in

Medellin and Colombia in general had influenced Andrés' decision to move to Europe and AC Milan at the end of the tournament. But before that he still realised the importance football could have on hopefully uniting the nation as they travelled to the 1994 World Cup.

If the build-up to the tournament had been tumultuous, then the opening game of the tournament did nothing to quell this. In separate interviews Andrés was asked more about issues at home rather than what lay ahead in the tournament. He spoke to the press about how they were trying not to focus on the violence, otherwise we can't play. In another how he reads the bible each day and thinks of the good times ahead. Former head of the Colombian Football Federation Juan Jose Bellini understood the importance that football had played," Amidst disaster, football played a vital role in restoring national pride". Bellini would later be locked up for 6 years for his role in money laundering for the Cali Cartel, when president of America de Cali. The team left as heroes, the President of the country Cesar Gavira called them personally to congratulate them and they also met with heads of state. The first fixture of the tournament took place on 19th June at the Rose Bowl. A crowd of 91,856 were present to see one of the much-lauded favourites in Colombia. Romania though was led by the mercurial talent Gheorghe Hagi, known as 'Regele' ('The King') to Romanian people. A relatively disappointing time at Real Madrid had many questioning whether his form at the Romanian based Steaua Bucharest was due to the standard in the league. A spell at Brescia in Italy had proven to people that he was as good as his early years shown. He was a standout player at the tournament and that would see him move to FC Barcelona at the end of the tournament. His skills were on show for everyone to see and Colombia were unable to stop the playmaker much to their despair. Higuita still in jail had been replaced by a relative novice, especially on the international stage by 23-year-old Oscar Cordoba of America de Cali. This would be his first major tournament, so many eyes were on him and how he would perform. Colombia started the stronger of the two sides fashioning a couple of half chances, but Romania's tactics were to stay compact and counterattack on the break. In the 15th minute AC Milan forward Florin Raducioiu produced a moment of brilliance. Picking the ball up on the edge of the box, beating two defenders before curling the ball into the far corner. Cordoba could do nothing to stop the goal, but the same could not be said for the next goal. On the 34th minute Hagi picked the ball up 35-yards out towards the touchline. It would take someone of his skill level to spot the keeper off his line, but also to attempt to score from this far out. Unfortunately for Cordoba he wasn't aware of Hagi's intentions and was left scrambling as the ball flew over his head and into the far corner. Cordoba later said, "It was my fault I lost sight of the ball, but he had struck it from 35 yards out".

Colombia was now chasing the game, and this fed directly into the hand of Romania and their counterattacking tactics. In the 44th minute they had some hope going into half time as Adolfo Valencia powered home a corner from a set piece. Colombia came out all guns blazing in the second half, Asprilla, Rincon and Valderrama wasting numerous chances. They would be punished again in the 89th minute chasing the game, as Hagi played a ball over the top of their defence. Cordoba trying his best to copy the style of his mentor Higuita came running of his line. Unfortunately for him this was the wrong decision as Raducioiu beat him to the ball and lifted the ball into the empty net. The tournament had got off to the worst possible start, but a sliver light was that Romania would be the strongest team they would face in the group stage and Hagi the best player.

Nobody could envisage the reaction to this defeat from back home. The country was a tinderbox ready to be ignited at any moment. The defeat seemed to have caused this to erupt if the preparations for the tournament were less than ideal. This was disastrous. For a must win game to remain in the tournament. Against the tournament hosts, with the backdrop of the US' drug war on their country. Firstly, Chonto Herrera's brother had been killed in Medellin the night after the game. This was said to be in a car accident, but the state of Medellin and the lawlessness in the state made some question the accident theory. The team waited for Herrera and gave him his news altogether. The measure of Andrés as a man and his nickname of the 'Gentleman of Football', as he comforted Herrera all night. But begged his defensive partner to stay, as they needed to win for their country and couldn't let them down.

The Cartels were waging a full-scale war. But the loss to Romania now turned some of their attentions to the team. Threats were made to the manager Francisco Maturana in his hotel room, that if he played defender Barrabas Gomez, that they would bomb their houses and they would kill members of the team too. The same calls were made personally to Gomez too and the assistant manager Hernan Dario. The players waited anxiously for Maturana and Dario for their team briefing in their hotel in Fullerton, California. What happened next would shock them all. Maturana came into the room crying, telling them all about the threats. He had made his decision for the team based on fear not football. He would heed the Cartels advice and drop Barrabas. Barrabas was distraught and retired instantly. The players then left the meeting and went to their rooms, to prepare for the biggest game of most careers to that date. They turned on their TVs to see the horror of the threats on all news outlets in Colombia. Faustino Asprilla in 30:30 said they went up and saw the threats

41

on TV. Every player was filled with worry. How was this anyway to prepare for a match.

Following Andrés own goal, his sister Maria remembers her 9-year-old son turning to her in the game and saying, "They're going to kill Andrés, aren't they?". The own goal had changed the flow of the game, with Colombia despite the off-field distractions coming closest to scoring. The US had nearly scored an own goal themselves, however, were fortunate to see theirs rebound off the post. The second half saw Earnie Stewart double the US' lead, with a late consolation goal from Valencia, being too little to late in their quest to remain in the tournament. This was seen as many of the sporting press as the biggest upset of the tournament. The much-fancied favourites had been beaten by a team here virtuoso of hosting the tournament, where football was relatively frowned upon by the public. Fans at home were furious at both the players but also those threatening the team. The cartel was enraged more, as many had backed the team with huge sums of money to do well at the tournament. A win in their final game against Switzerland was all in vain, as they finished bottom of the group. Maturana announced his decision to step away the team, disillusioned by the state of his country. He begged the players to stay in the US for their own safety, as Medellin burned. Andrés was offered a punditry role by Caracol, for the rest of the tournament, however he didn't think this was right after what had happened in the tournament. He had a holiday to Vegas booked to visit family but decided to cancel this and return home. He was upset that he had scored an own goal but felt this was purely a mistake. He was loved in Medellin, why should he be ashamed and hideaway. His goal had been a mistake, one he had never intended to make, but the biggest mistake he would make, was returning to Medellin.

"I never heard any of the players say we were going to win the World Cup or get to the final. At most, we could have got one or two rounds further, that would have been fair", Oscar Cortes a member of Colombia's 1994 World Cup Squad. The team although confident, didn't believe they would win the tournament. The win over Argentina had caused others to label them as favourites. This weighed heavily on the players and brought embarrassment to them all when they were knocked out in the group stages. The players and Andrés had wanted to unite the country, make their people proud and go some way to repair their international image. The events 10 days post-embarrassing defeat at the hands of the US and Andrés unfortunate own goal, would destroy any progress they had made post-Pablo's death and worse than prior to his death. On 2nd July 1994, Andrés made the fateful decision to have a night out with close friends. His fiancé asked him to reconsider, but he didn't want to hide away. He loved the people of Medellin, and they loved him. He visited a few clubs before attending El Indio nightclub. It was here that three men began to heckle Andrés referring to the own goal. Andrés tried to reason with the men before deciding to leave the nightclub. Andrés got in his car to drive away, but the men had followed him outside. He drove over to the men again, trying to reason with them. The argument got heated, as one of the three men then pulled out a 38. calibre revolver shooting Andrés six times. Each time he was shoot the shooter reportedly shouted, "Gol". Andrés would be rushed to hospital but died 45 minutes later.

Andrés' love of football and loyalty to his country had got him killed. Even after his death the links to Pablo Escobar continued. Although, the police couldn't prove direct Cartel involvement, many believe this was due to the influence of corrupted officers. The car that drove away from the scene of the murder was registered to the Gallon brothers. Pedro and Santiago Gallon were two of the three men who were arguing with Andrés. Both were once linked to the Medellin Cartel but now worked under the wings of Carlos Castano, founder of 'Los Pepes'. Although, their jobs were reputedly 'coffee growers' and 'sports apparel sellers', they were known drug traffickers. Murder was a common thing in Colombia, but this murder shocked not only the Colombian public but the whole world. Someone who had played at the biggest tournament in world football only ten days before now lay dead in a mortuary. The Gallon brothers would never be convicted of the murder, instead their bodyguard Humberto Castro Munoz, would be convicted of murder. Rumours to this day are rife, for the reasons why. Some say the brothers had lost $3million dollars betting on Colombia in the World Cup. Others that Andrés had disrespected them during the heat of the argument. Most not believing the story it was their bodyguard of his own accord shooting Andrés, without either orders or taking the flack for one of the brothers. Carlos Castano was very powerful and able to influence prosecutors, something Andrés family still believe to this day. The sentences served support that, Munoz sentenced to 43 years in prison only served 11 years. Whilst the brothers convicted of assisting an offender received one year suspended sentences. The links to Pablo continued for Andrés even to his death, although not killed by the same shooter, both deaths were linked to the same crime group 'Los Pepes'.

There was outrage and grief, as up to 100,000 people lined the streets of Medellin to see the beloved son of their city. His body lay in state at the Medellin basketball arena. A sea of green and white (Atletico Nacional colours) visited over the coming days, with 15,000 present to see him lowered into his final resting place. President Gavira asked for calm and tolerance, but although his war on drugs had taken out the biggest drug dealer in the world. He had created a power vacuum that had now cost the life of an innocent man, who was trying to use football as a vehicle for change. His coach Francisco Maturana rightly pointed out: *"Our society believed that soccer killed Andrés, Andrés was a soccer player killed by society "*. In 2018 his sister Maria shared what many believe to be true about football. "Football should be a vehicle of peace and social transformation, and at the end of the day, it is just a game". This was echoed by Andrés throughout his life as a footballer. The famous Bill Shankly quote says that football is much more important than life or death. He didn't mean that so matter-of-factly. Unfortunately for Andrés a mistake in a football match had cost him his life. The sport he and so many other Colombians loved so much, would lead to his death, although not directly.

2
Performance-Enhancing Drugs

"If you take me back to 1995, when doping was completely pervasive, I would probably do it again."

Lance Armstrong
Interview with BBC in 2015

It's probably a little strange starting a chapter in a book all about football with a quote from a Cyclist. The reason it was chosen is because of the honesty shown by Armstrong in his interview with the BBC for his documentary 'Lance'. Although the doping he took part in was systematic and was anything but honest. However, he is one of the only sportspeople to come out and admit his use of performance-enhancing drugs. In a 2013 interview he admitted to using testosterone and human growth hormone, as well as EPO. All this to increase the amount of oxygen that can be delivered to his muscles and improving his recovery/endurance. When news broke it was one of, if not the biggest sporting scandal of all-time. Armstrong had been an inspiration to millions around the world. Recovering from cancer to win the toughest race in the world. But not just once but seven consecutive times between 1999-2005. Something that had never been done before and may never be done again. He was one of the most recognisable sportspeople in the world, not just for his sporting prowess. The money he raised through his 'Livestrong' foundation has raised upwards of $500 million for cancer research.

His reputation was ruined, after years of denying the accusations (dating back to 2005), he finally admitted to his crimes. Some say he didn't have any choice as the evidence piled up. But what is so rare is for someone to come out and admit their guilt. The reason he used performance-enhancing drugs. To win. He told Le Monde in 2013 "It's impossible to win the Tour de France without doping". The United States Anti-Doping Agency (USADA) found he had used performance-enhancing drugs throughout his career. They called it in their report "the most sophisticated, professionalized and successful doping programme that sport has ever seen".

Armstrong felt he had to do it to win, because his argument was that everyone was doing it. Teddy Cutler of SportIntelligence.com took a detailed look at all the top cyclists from 1998-2005 (The period of Armstrong's proven doping). He found that of the 81 different riders who finished in the top-10 over this period, 65% have been caught doping. Cycling has a systematic issue with doping, one that it still has some way to clean up.

But back to football. Although in no way shape or form is doping in football close to the level found in cycling. Not even that in America's biggest sport, American Football. Where around 1% of players were found to use PED's. However, USA Today Sports reported that they believe the sport has a problem like cycling. Where the admitted dopers avoid testing positive in tests.

That doesn't mean football is immune to doping. Between 2013-2020, 88 footballers from England, Wales and Scotland failed doping tests, returning 'adverse analytical findings.' More worrying, was a 'The Mail on Sunday' investigation, that found out of these 88 positive tests, at least 15 were Premier League footballers. 12 of the 15 positive tests were for banned performance-enhancing substances. The worrying part. NONE of those players received any kind of ban. The UK Anti-Doping agency (UKAD) made obtaining this information particularly difficult for their investigation too, forcing the paper to make a series of Freedom of Information requests. This leads some to believe some form of cover-up. The fact that all players identities are also withheld, as it might compromise UKAD's investigative functions. But also, a rather strange reason, 'the protection of minors'. The reason given for the players not being banned by UKAD, was accidental ingestion or the player having a Therapeutic Use Exemption (TUE).

Of the PED's found in the 12 positive cases:
- One positive test for an amphetamine
- Three positive tests of Triamcinolone. This was a drug used by Bradley Wiggins during Tour De France victory. Although he had a TUE for this. However, a parliamentary investigation found he had crossed an 'ethical' line.
- Four positives for the stimulant Ritalin. This is a drug used to treat ADHD but can also improve performance. Simone Biles, the Olympic Gold medallist in gymnastics, had a TUE for its use in 2016. But in 2020, her US Gymnast teammate Shawn Johnson, also a gold medallist. Said she had been prescribed another ADHD drug (Adderall) to aid weight loss and give her more energy. Ritalin has also been found to be abused in Cycling and MMA.
- The others were for steroids prednisolone and a derivative. There was also a positive test for diuretic indapamide, which is used for weight loss but also as a masking agent for other banned substances.

39 of the 88 positive tests were itemised by UKAD as PED's. Of the other 24 non-premier league, 15 ended up with bans ranging from 3 months to 4 years. The only case of a Premier League club having a player banned for using a PED, was a 15-year-old registered to a premier league club. In October 2019, the child was found with a banned growth hormone-dispensing pen, which resulted in a nine-month ban.

It must therefore be presumed that the Premier League players all have TUE's. But why is that not the case for the player's outside the Premier League? Have players found a way round these positive tests by using TUE's? But UKAD and the FA found there is no proof of any wrongdoing and are happy with the evidence produced by the players and teams. The 12 PED cases had innocent explanations and therefor no punishment was taken. 12 of the 15 positive tests from the Premier League was for PED's as we have discussed above. Therefore, we must presume that the other 3 tests were for recreational/social drugs. We will look at that aspect in more detail later.

Positive tests however have not always gone unpunished. Some of the World's biggest stars over the years have been involved in PED scandals. None however have come out and admitted they did this to gain an advantage and help them to win. All still to this day deny that they did this in their quest to win at all costs. All 'accidentally' ingested the drugs through tainted supplements/food. Let's look at some of the most famous cases:

Players Banned for using PED's

Diego Maradona-1994

The iconic picture seen by everybody around the world. Diego Maradona, staring manically into the camera, as he screamed releasing the frustration he had felt since the 1990 World Cup. The 1994 US World Cup was memorable not just for the quality of football. The death of Andres Escobar also left a dark cloud over the tournament. But the failure of a drug test for 5 banned substances on FIFA's banned substances list, by arguably the greatest player of his generation, shocked the world. Was everyone surprised he had failed a drug test? Not really, considering a lengthy ban in 1991 for a positive test for Cocaine (more on this later). However, it was the fact it wasn't cocaine and a PED that shocked so many. After defeating Italy in the 1990 World Cup hosted by Italy, in the semi-finals. The Italian media had turned against Maradona, his safe haven in Naples was now ruined. He tested positive for cocaine in 1991 resulting in a 15-month ban from football. After that an unsuccessful spell at Seville in La Liga, were his issues with cocaine didn't stop. This was now affecting his ability on the pitch now. His mercurial ability seemed to be dwindling, which wasn't supported by his poor fitness levels. He returned to Argentina, signing for Rosario based Newell's Old Boys. But still there he seemed to be nearing the end of his career. He was 33 and seriously unfit, struggling to keep up with the pace of the game in the Argentinian domestic league. The 1994 World Cup must've been nothing but a pipe dream. But then came the earth-shattering defeat to Columbia in Argentina's last World Cup qualifier. They were embarrassed, the team were labelled a disgrace. So out went the Bat-Signal. The fans called for 'El Diego's' return to the national team. No matter his domestic form, their famous number 10 was the only person they felt could resurrect their World Cup dreams. Their prayers were answered, he was returned the squad for the two-legged playoff versus Australia. The winner would qualify for the World Cup.

He made an instant impact in the first leg. Assisting Argentina's only goal in a 1-1 draw in Australia. The return leg was a cagey affair, however Argentina scraped through with an own goal sealing a 1-0 victory. They were on their way to the 1994 World Cup, but Maradona had now left Newell's. He had no club, and his fitness couldn't match that of his teammates. He made the decision to have a make-or-break fitness camp, that would last one week. He would push his body to it's limits with high intensity training, surrounded by a team of fitness specialists. He was reported to lose 12kg and decided he had made enough progress to be near some level of fitness near to his teammates. Argentina would have their talisman for one last World Cup.

Argentina had been written off by most of the world media in the build-up to the tournament. The 5-0 defeat to Columbia still fresh in everyone's minds. Maradona wasn't the only player returning from a drug ban. Another star player for the team, Claudio Caniggia was returning from his own 13-month drug ban too. The team would therefore you'd think would be under increased scrutiny from FIFA's drug testers. The celebration seen and replayed by so many after the failed drug test, somewhat trying to show his guilt due to the bulging eyes, came in their first game. Maradona playing a deeper role pulling the strings and feeding the dangerous strike force at Argentina's disposal silenced their critics. A hat-trick from Gabriel Batistuta, was followed by a goal a prime Maradona would've been proud of. A curling effort with his famous left-foot gave the Greece keeper now chance as it nestled in the top corner. The 4-0 win made the world media sit up and take notice. The following game Maradona was pivotal again, dictating the game for Argentina. He assisted Caniggia for one of his two goals, also silencing his doubters following his previous failed test. They defeated the talented Nigerians 2-1 putting them top of their group with 6 point and wins in both games.

Then came the moment that would take the wind out of Argentina's briming sails. But also shock the whole world. After the Nigeria game, Maradona was taken for a post-match drug test. The day before their final group game against Bulgaria, Maradona was informed of the results of his positive test. He denied all the allegations. The AFA president Julio Grodona met with the world's press not long after. He told the press that the Ephedrine had been found due to a nasal spray Maradona had used, one that is bought over the counter in Argentina. Dr Michael d'Hooghe a FIFA committee member denied the possibility of this outright. Pointing out that the other substances found in the positive test weren't in the nasal spray, further remarking no product contained all of them together. The second test came back positive as well. The man who had lit up the World Cup, would bow out on the biggest stage marred in disgrace. He was sent home by the AFA. Argentina now Maradona-less would have to find a way to keep the momentum he had created. The ban was like a pin popping a balloon full of all Argentina's charisma and confidence. They lost the final group game 2-0 against Bulgaria. Meaning even after their two wins they finished third in the group. This setup a tie with Romania. A game some describe as the best and most exciting game of the whole tournament. None of which will bring Argentina any comfort, losing 3-2, to the Gheroge Hagi led Romania. A tournament before Maradona's return that didn't have much hope, had been ignited by his return. Only to be extinguished as soon as the results were proven by the second test. For their worst performance since 1982, exiting in the last-16.

Still Maradona strenuously denied the results of the drug test. Saying he had never taken PED's. He blamed it on a witch-hunt by AFA President Julio Grodona and FIFA, trying to tarnish his name. Somewhat changing from his previous stance of a nasal spray. He then turned to blaming one of his fitness trainers who had given him an American supplement that contained Ephedrine, unbeknown to his knowledge. He was banned for 15-months. His triumphant return had ended in tears. "They've (Fifa) cut my legs off. This is a real dirty business. I'd like to believe in Joao Havelange and Sepp Blatter but after this…. Well, I don't want to say anything". Was Maradona's response to the media in the immediate aftermath, reiterating his claims of a conspiracy. FIFA however did support his views that he hadn't taken them consciously to improve performance. That was the responsibility of Daniel Cerrini, a bodybuilder who had supported his return to fitness. He was also banned for 15 months. It was however a tragedy for one of the world's most revered footballers of all-time for talent shown. Unfortunately, his demons and issues with drugs mean many didn't give him any benefit of the doubt.

Edgar Davids, Ronald De Boer and Jaap Stam-2001

2001 was a challenging year for three of the Netherland's top players. The timing couldn't be worse. The Oranje were amid a qualification battle for the 2002 World Cup. One that would ultimately result in them missing out on qualification, losing out to the Republic of Ireland. All the disruption to the three players at the centre of a drug scandal could've played some part in their issues. Edgar Davids at the time played for Juventus. At the time it was said many of the top Premier League sides were courting him during the 2001 season, with a potential summer transfer. Ronald de Boer was at the time playing for FC Barcelona. Having played over 172 games for Ajax during their period of winning the

Champions League and multiple Eredevise titles. The last was Jaap Stam, who in his 3 years at Manchester United was part of their famous treble winning side. Some believe he was one of the greatest centre backs of the Premier League era. This all ended acrimoniously though, due to comments about how the club was ran in his autobiography 'Head to Head'. He also shared views on opposing players. This reportedly upset Sir Alex Ferguson and he had been sold to Lazio that summer for £16 million. Ferguson did deny this though and would later say it was due to believing he wouldn't recover from an Achilles injury, something he later admitted was a mistake.

The reason the three players have been grouped together to discuss their use of PED's, is that all tested positive for Nandrolone. All also tested positive around the same period of 2000-2001. Nandrolone is an anabolic steroid. The effects it has on an athlete is to increase muscle strength and mass. It also speeds up recovery of an athlete after taking part in physical activity. The maximum permissible value for men is 2.0 nanograms per ml. De Boer tested positive after a UEFA Cup quarter final for FC Barcelona versus Celta Vigo. His reading was four times above the permissible value, with an 8.6 reading. His Oranje and former Ajax teammate Davids tested positive after a Serie A game against Udinese. However, his was only slightly over at 2.7. Stam's test came slightly after his national teammates, but he also tested positive with a reading of 5.5.

The fact that three players from the same national team had tested positive for the same drug created suspicion around how this could be possible. The first line of enquiry was vitamin pills they had been given by the medical team from the Dutch national team. All the players in question had taken the vitamin pills on international duty. Another was that it had come from tainted food eaten by the players. Their Dutch international teammate Bert Konterman blamed the whole issue on Dutch Farmers. He suggested that the cattle they produced are injected with Nandrolone and this is how the players had come to test positive. What furthered the suspicions about the vitamin supplement though was the negative tests returned by De Boer's National and club teammates Phillip Cocu and Patrick Kluivert. The reason for this was that they didn't take the exact same tablet. The reason for this is that they struggled to swallow big tablets. Instead, they were given an effervescent tablet variant due to their issues ingesting the other tablets. This raised the question that they had tested negative due to not receiving the same tablet. All three players strenuously denied they had willingly used PED's. However, after testing positive first, De Boer took the fight to clear his name more thoroughly than the others.

De Boer was initially banned for one year. This ban strangely only applied to International Matches. Therefore, it would affect his participation in important qualifiers for the World Cup. De Boer spent a fortune to clear his innocence. He used his own money to ask specialists and lawyers from around the world for advice. During this period another theory arose, that his positive test was due to a Salve he had given his daughter. But this didn't explain the positive tests of Davids and Stam. It was also argued by scientists that the levels the players tested positive for cannot be described as doping. An example they used to explain their reasoning for this were the levels of Athletes banned for the use of Nandrolone. Linford Christie is an example that can be used to compare. When he tested positive for Nandrolone, his levels were 200. This is 100 times the permissible value, and is what scientists believe is evidence of systematic doping. Not just the accidental ingestion of a tainted supplement. To further prove his innocence, he gave hair samples to drug testers. These tests could not prove that he had consciously doped. Due to the effort that De Boer had put into proving he was not a doper, FIFA reversed their original decision. It was decided he had unknowingly taken Nandrolone through a contaminated food supplement. His ban was reduced to 11 weeks.

In an interview with Voetbal International chief editor Johan Derksen, when asked about the issues in 2001 he said this. "Yes, lawyers – we've been everywhere. In the end I've spend 750.000 to 1.000.000 gulden (62,000 euros-80,000 euros) in this case and in the end you're still guilty. But on the other hand, you're not guilty, because they have given you two and a half months until you could return for the important world cup qualifier match against Ireland. But they could not find me not guilty, because otherwise they needed to declare everyone not guilty. It is like bringing water into the sea."

De Boer had done the groundwork for his international teammates. Davids and Stam were both banned for five months. Although this was longer than De Boer, in comparison to players in Serie A banned at the same time, it was lenient. Fernando Couto a Portuguese international and Lazio centre back was banned in the same period for ten months. His levels were lower than that of Stam's at 4.6, showing the Dutch players, particularly Stam had been looked on favourably.

Pep Guardiola-2001

Maradona in my opinion is the biggest name on this list. From a football perspective from what he achieved on the pitch. But also, for his 'godlike' existence for Argentines and Neapolitans. For the younger generation Guardiola however will be the most recognisable name on this list. They know him as a manager who has redefined how football is played. Adapting the philosophy of his master Johan Cruyff, to produce a possession-based style of football, that allows his teams to dominate the opposition. His teams have also dominated the Spanish, German and English domestic leagues and cups. This style of football allowed His FC Barcelona team from 2008-2012 dominate world football. That team will go down as one of the best teams of all time. In his first season as manager, they won a historic treble. Winning La Liga, the Copa del Rey and the Champions League, defeating a Cristiano Ronaldo led Manchester United. In doing so they became the first Spanish team to ever achieve the feat. Guardiola also became the youngest manager to win the champions league ever in doing so. He would win the champions league again in 2011, as well as winning the league. Once again, they defeated Manchester United in the champions league final at Wembley, in what many believe was the most complete footballing performance of all time. After 4 years he took a break from managing after winning a record breaking 14 trophies in that time. Although in Germany and England he hasn't achieved the same European success. He has dominated domestically. Winning 3 consecutive Bundesliga's in his 3 years with Bayern München. Whilst also winning 4 out of 5 premier leagues with Manchester City, where he has also won a domestic treble.

However, what some of the younger generation forget about Pep is that he isn't just a excellent manager. As a player he was a key cog in Cruyff's dream team of the early 90s. Playing as the 'pivot' behind the talents of Stoichkov, Laudrup and Romario to name a few. In 1997 he was made captain by Louis Van Gaal. After being at the club from the age of 13, and playing 12 seasons for the first team, winning 16 trophies. He decided he needed a change, due to injuries that had plagued his last few years and the speed of the game. Guardiola would be a hero for many of the next generation, including 3 of his most important players as manager of Barca in Xavi, Iniesta and Fabregas. At the age of 30, in 2001 he left Barca to sign for Brescia in Serie a. He would be the deep lying playmaker who would replace a young departing, Andrea Pirlo. He would be playing alongside a fading Roberto Baggio.

Now I know the last section sounded like de Boer was fully exonerated of any wrongdoing based on the information presented. Apologies if this next section leaves you questioning that slightly. But like with all parts of this book, I am just presenting information. I am not the judge and the jury. You can come to your own conclusions and decisions based on what is presented. Now there is quite a few things that link de Boer and Guardiola both:

1. Played for Barca in their career.
2. Were managed and highly thought of by van Gaal.
3. Played in similar positions, deep lying in the midfield.
4. Were also trained in the football philosophy of Cruyff.

However, what also links them and some further things to do with this. Is that they both tested positive for nandrolone.

In the same period as the Dutch trio. Guardiola also tested positive whilst playing in serie a, just like Stam and Davids. Guardiola gave two samples on two separate occasions, that both tested positive for nandrolone. Firstly, after a game against Piacenza on 21st October. The second was against Lazio away in the studio Olimpico on 4th November 2001. Both times the test were above the permissible level, around 8-9ml were Guardiola's positive tests. The Italian league banned him for 4 months and fined him €50,000. He was also required to submit random drug tests for 4 months during his ban. Another similarity he had with de Boer is that he didn't believe the positive tests and protested his innocence, appealing the ban. Upon his first appeal the Football's federal court of justice upheld the ban. During the appeal Guardiola denied willingly taking PED's. He said that the only supplements he took were multi-vitamins that he took off his trusted personal physiologist Dr Ramon Seguera. He said he had taken supplements for 6/7 years and he had never returned a positive test during that time, taking some 60 tests. Here is another link between de Boer and Guardiola. Dr Ramon Seguera was also physician to de Boer during his time at Barca. Seguera went to court to argue the supplements he had given Guardiola were contaminated and this had caused the positive test. However, the court tested all these supplements and none of them showed any traces of nandrolone. The court were also critical of his methods of sourcing supplements, describing them as 'risky'.

Things got worse for Guardiola. The court of Brescia now started legal proceedings against him. Due to changes in Italian law in 2000, it was now a criminal offence to dope in sport. Guardiola was given a 7-month suspended sentence, a €9000 fine and ordered to pay the legal fees of the prosecution. During this court case, Guardiola used a new doctor to protest his innocence. Dr Jordi Segura testified the positive test was due to Guardiola having Gilbert syndrome. This is a condition that can lead to jaundice (yellowing of the skin). The doctor argued due to this syndrome the body had naturally produced the cells through hormones in his body. The court however ruled this out.

Finally, though in 2007 he cleared his name. Unlike de Boer however he was able to clear his name fully and be exonerated of doping. How this come about is his personal assistant and close friend Manuel Estiarte, a former professional water polo player. Found a change in the World Anti-Doping Agency's (WADA's) guidelines. In 2005, he had read about a new phenomenon in testing called 'unstable urine'. This was when tests could lead to positive tests for low levels of nandrolone; due to a chemical reaction in a vial containing urine. WADA director general at the time, David Howman stood by the testing though. He stated that it was very rare for this to happen. With the chances being between 1 In a 1000 to 1 in 10,000, where unstable urine would cause a positive test. This makes the chances of it happening in two separate tests even rarer than those chances.

But due to these new changes, Guardiola was cleared by Brescia court of appeals. Not because there was definitive proof that his tests were unstable. But because stability tests need to take place within 5 weeks of the original sample being taken. So due to the period being well over this, some 6 years. They couldn't prove his tests were unstable but couldn't prove that they weren't either. Italian anti-doping prosecutors appealed this in 2009, saying that the tests were conducted correctly, and this wasn't new evidence. They also argued, why this defence hadn't been used in the first two appeals. They were not happy that he had been allowed to appeal for a third time either. Their appeal however was rejected though. Guardiola was exonerated and unlike the others had managed in a court of law to change his ruling to prove he was now 'innocent'.

Back to de Boer again though, who like Guardiola we have pointed out, has fought tooth and nail to prove his innocence. The supplements that he and the other Dutch players ingested on Holland duty were platina multi-Vitamin pills from Ortho company. After thorough testing on the multi-vitamins, it showed no traces of Nandrolone. The company who produced the multi-vitamins were rightly angered about having their product brandished as being contaminated and threatened legal action against de Boer. This meant he was no longer allowed to talk about the vitamins he had been given on Holland duty in relation to doping. That probably explains this 2013 quote from the same interview with Voetball.

"No. The only explanation we had were vitamin pills we received from the KNVB, but those had a safe reputation. That was what we wanted, that's what the KNVB wanted. The doctor underlined explicitly that those drugs were also used by the Dutch national volleyball team. Those would be safe and got controlled frequently I believe around the Olympic games. That's why we took these pills. I don't say these drugs were it in the end, because it could have been in beef for example, too."

Like I have said, I am not the judge and jury. We will never have a definitive answer for what caused the positive nandrolone tests. It could have been Dr Segura's special tablets. Maybe it was some of the contaminated Dutch meat, Guardiola might have been partial to it too. They all could have suffered from jaundice caused by Gilbert Syndrome. Or some degree of impossibility, all unfortunately had 'unstable urine samples' which have caused them to test positive. What I alluded to at the start of this chapter is that although he is not linked to football, lance Armstrong is rare, as he openly admits he dopped to win. He wanted to seek an advantage over his other competitions that would allow him to win at all costs. We may never know what caused the positive tests of the players as a cloud of doubt surrounds all the possibilities. But whether the players took them willingly or people they trusted give them to them to give them an advantage. It could be true that it was a contaminated food supplement/ product that no parties knew about. But if they did know this proves the lengths some would go to, to win and gain an advantage over others. Anabolic steroids can cause lots of serious long term health effects. These are all very worrying but so are the mental affects it can have on the person taking:

- Paranoia
- Extreme irritability and rage
- Delusions and false belief
- Impaired judgment
- Mania

So, if they or people they trust have willingly give them the drugs, is winning/ being better in football worth that. This is without even thinking about the long term affects. The mental pressures of football are enough to cause mental health issues. But if they feel steroids will help them to overcome issues in their performance, is that more important than their mental health and long-term health. Until a player comes out and says they have openly doped to help them succeed, then we may not know the whole thought process behind their decision. But it has certainly left a black mark on some of the best footballers of their generation. Players whose natural talent has made them stand out above the rest, may have felt they never had any other option. What is interesting in Maradona's case is how open he is to admit his recreational drug use. This is because he knows it didn't make him a better player. It hindered him. So, either he truthfully had no knowledge, or the players are embarrassed to let others know they don't think their talent can make them stand out above the rest any longer. The embarrassment of that overrides the decision making when it comes to affecting their body and mind, they can't let that advantage they have go.

3
Recreational drugs

"Those who say cocaine stimulates you don't know a thing. If you take cocaine to play football, you can't play. It's not good for being on the pitch. It's useless for life. Useless."

Diego Maradona in 1996 speaking to Gente Magazine

This chapter will look at bans related to recreational drug taking from footballers. Recreational drugs such as: Cocaine, Cannabis and Ecstasy/MDMA, to name a few, are all prohibited substances in sports. The reason giving by WADA, is that these drugs are perceived to be performance enhancing. Like Maradona pointed out in his 1996 interview, cocaine doesn't help you when you play football. Like all the recreational drugs that are on the banned list, for them to be deemed to be performance enhancing is ridiculous. Everybody in life has probably come across someone taking recreational drugs or experimented themselves. The common cocaine user in the pub, chatting the ear off anyone who will listen, being over friendly hugging anyone they encounter. WADA must think this will aid defenders too much, marshalling the back four and tight man marking. Your regular stoner, you smell them before you see them, on the hunt for food as the munchies kick in. This is obviously a no go; we can't make strikers hungrier for goals than they already are. Your 18–21-year-old taking ecstasy tablets in a club, sweating profusely but excellent non-stop two-stepping. This added energy must be a must for any midfielder if their jaw swinging doesn't distract them too much and they stay hydrated.

Maradona is one of the greatest players of all time and was never shy in declaring how good he was in comparison to other greats. But even his self-belief waned due to his cocaine use. In 2014 he told Argentina's Tyc Sports, "I gave my opponents a big advantage due to my illness. Do you know the player I could have been if I hadn't taken drugs?". For a person who is thought of as 'God' in his own country, the regret he has towards his cocaine use is telling. In no way shape or form did it give him an advantage when playing football. In Maradona's biography he talked about his early experiences of using cocaine. "I tried it in Europe for the first time in 1982," he said. "I was 22 years old; it was enough for me to feel alive. I tried drugs because there are drugs like that everywhere in football." This was denied by many of his friends at the time who said he first tried the drug the night he celebrated leaving Barca to join Napoli. It was given to him by his father-in-law Roque Nicolas Villafane. He initially loved it because it didn't stop him winning, but soon that left for loneliness, fear and doubt.

To try to overcome this he continued to use the drug for the whole time he was at Napoli trying to find the original high. Naples was looked down on by the industrial north. Known as 'terrone', meaning from the land. His first match against Verona saw them show a banner saying, 'Welcome to Italy'. Showing how they didn't perceive the south to be part of Italy. Maradona adhered himself to the Neapolitans straight away, using La domencia Sportiva. "There is a racism problem in Italian football but not against black people. There is racism is against Neapolitans and that is a disgrace". The first home game the fans unveiled a banner in his honour. "Uno Di noi"- one of us. He was with them: and he was with them in their fight against the rest of the country. Issues began in Naples when he fell out with his long-term advisor Jorge Cyterszpiler over money. He became untrustworthy even though all he had done was try to protect him. In his place came a new agent, Guillermo Coppola. A yes man who would also take drugs with him. He was loved by the people of Naples, the club and was also a friend of the Camorra, meaning he was protected for a long period of time at Napoli. His use of Cocaine spiralled out of control though when a paternity scandal was made public knowledge. He had fathered a child to a woman he had a brief affair with, but denied that the child was his, forcing the woman to release this to the press. This rocked Maradona and his wife and family but continued to deny the child was his. The people of Naples threatened the family and even the mayor of Naples condemned them all concerned about Maradona wanting to leave. This caused his mood to change however, cocaine was no longer just a distraction. He lost the shine in his eyes and his mood changed. It got so bad that he would take it in toilet as his daughter would try to come in. People were dropping deliveries off in the middle of the night to the house and he would continue to deny what was going on to his wife. Some days his wife would leave him all day in bed.

He had fell into a deep depression and his use of cocaine was accelerating this. The pressure of living in Naples where he was mobbed everywhere he went and being the talisman of the team made his time in Naples turn into a nightmare. Even throughout this period he managed to help Napoli secure the Serie A title and lift the UEFA Cup, their first ever major European trophy. Throughout this period though he missed training staying in his house using cocaine and making excuses for why he wasn't there. The whole time he was spied on by club president Corrado Ferlaino and director Luciano Moggi. They listened to the reports but did nothing to help his addiction, Ferlaino said this, "From Sunday night to Wednesday, Diego was free to do what he wanted. But on Thursday he had to be clean". At the time his weekly routine was described as this:

Sunday: Serie A match.
Sunday night to Wednesday: continuous cocaine binge, usually with Camorra.
Wednesday morning to Saturday: "cleanse" and sweat it all out.
Sunday: Serie A match.

If he ever overdid this, then the club were also known to use over player's urine to pass the tests if needed. But this was done on a weekly basis, unless a big game was coming up or an important part of the season. The he would manage to stay clean for a period to get himself fit as possible. For many years Maradona tried to leave Napoli and came close on a few occasions to joining Marseille and Bernard Tapie. Napoli however backed out numerous times on promises made to Maradona that they would allow him to leave, most prominently after winning a second Serie A title and the UEFA cup. Maradona was eventually banned in 1991, when he was banned for 15 months by Napoli for testing positive for cocaine – this lasted from April 1991 – June 1992. Before this though his relationship with the club and Naples (including the Mafia) had broken down anyway. It was difficult times for mafia and because of his links to prostitutes controlled by the mafia, he was dragged into an operation against the Camorra. He was implicated as they had wire taps on hookers and through these wiretaps he was caught asking for coke or mentioning it. Five prostitutes declared he had given them cocaine and he was charged with use and distribution of cocaine by the Neapolitan courts. He was given fourteen months, but it was suspended and also fined 4 million lira. December 1990 saw him fined $70000 by the Federcalcio and Napoli due to damaging the club's image due to the court case. He had 2 and a half years left on his contract, but he was saying he was going Boca and the club wanted him gone too. Maradona had fell out of love with the people of Naples at the time too, for how they treated him after defeating Italy in the semi-finals of the Italia 90 World Cup The positive test then gave them the reason, they needed to get rid of him without a massive payoff. "I tested positive almost on purpose. Yes, on purpose I wanted it". He admitted to journalist Daniel Arcucci some years later.

Later in the same year he was arrested in Buenos Aires for possessing half-kilo of cocaine and was given a 14-month suspended sentence. In this time, he was in Buenos Aires supposedly to enter rehab and try to solve his cocaine issue. He moved to his old team Boca Juniors in 1995 via a short but relatively unsuccessful stint at Sevilla. However, in 1997 he failed a drug test for the third time in six years putting an end to his playing career. This failure was only ever described officially as due to 'prohibited substances' although Boca president Mauricio Macri said he was told cocaine had been present in a urine sample. Even before this final ban, Maradona told a drugs charity in 1996: 'Drugs are everywhere, and I do not want kids to take them. 'I have two girls and I thought it best to say this, a father's obligation... I was, am and always will be a drug addict.'

English football has also had issues with recreational drug use though. Professor Ivan Waddington is a professor at the University of Chester, who has decades of experience studying the use of drugs in sport. He has conducted various studies where professional footballers have answered anonymous survey. This anonymity allowed the players to be truthful and reveal the issues football has with recreational drug taking. He said that his studies showed that drug taking is, "widespread". The most common drugs being used were marijuana and cocaine. Waddington blamed the FA and the clubs for the high levels he found through his survey. "I don't think the FA takes drug testing as seriously as it ought to- it will deny this of course" Waddington concluded. "And I certainly don't think the football clubs take drug testing as seriously as they ought to. And again, individual clubs will deny that". The last chapter it was mentioned about the 15 failed tests from Premier League players in a 7-year period (2013-2020). We know 12 of these tests were for PED's, so therefore must presume the other 3 were for recreational drugs. 39 of the 88 positive drug tests across England and Scotland in all leagues were PED's. So, the majority (49 of 88) must have been recreational drugs. When asked UKAD declined to itemise these due to the FA telling UKAD, 'It would not be acceptable' to release details on cases involving social drugs that are banned by WADA but not by the FA.

This is due to the FA dealing separately to WADA regulations when it comes to Recreational/Social drugs. The FA's stance is: **"The purpose of The FA Social Drugs Regulations is to prevent the damaging consequences to the health and welfare of Players and/or of those who regard Players as role models, and also to protect the image and reputation of the sport, by providing courses of education, counselling and treatment, where appropriate, to rehabilitate Players who have become involved with Social Drugs."**
Personally, I think this is the correct way to deal with positive tests related to recreational drugs. How is banning players from playing the sport they love, going to help them kick a drug habit. It's clear it doesn't give them an advantage, so supporting them and keeping their identities anonymous will also help the player. But the FA also state in the same policy:
"Remember, if a Player breaches the Social Drug Regulations they may also receive a ban from Football so it

is important that all Participants understand the dangers of social drugs"
I will talk about some of the cases that have led to players receiving such bans, the reason seems to be when the players tested positively. If the test takes place during training/at the players club, then it is dealt with in-house with the FA and the rehabilitation programme. However, if the positive test occurs during a match, this has then resulted in bans. This change in policy is therefore down to the clear performance enhancing advantages of having these social drugs in your system for the match. To me this seems crazy, why are the players treated differently, when it's clear it hasn't helped them in any way. Why are these players punished more severely and not given the support they need. In a few of these publicised cases the players are left out to dry by the FA and there is no duty of care for the player's mental health or future career.

The first reported ban for the use of social drugs was in 1995. The player in question was Chris Armstrong. Armstrong was a star of the inaugural Premier League season, scoring 23 goals in his first season for the South-London club. He then had the inauspicious award of being the first Premier League player to fail a drug test in 1995. Armstrong, unlike his namesake 'Lance', didn't test positive for PED's but cannabis. He was given a one month ban by the FA and ordered to take part in a rehabilitation course. In fairness to the media at the time, they were quite strong in their defence of Armstrong. Like I have above pointed out the fact it clearly doesn't improve performance. They also felt it was the least harmful of supposed social drugs in comparison to cocaine and heroin. The Independent's anger at the time stemmed from the unfair treatment he received compared to other cases of "bringing the game into disrepute". They listed the fact that Chelsea's Dennis Wise had received no ban for assaulting a taxi-driver or

Vinnie Jones who had bitten a man's nose in a Dublin hotel. It was clear that Armstrong had done no harm to anyone, unlike the two incidents above or had he sought to cheat. Therefore, his treatment correctly they highlighted was unfair.

Fortunately for Armstrong it didn't affect his career to significantly. That same year Tottenham made him their record signing at the time for £4.5 million. He won the league cup with Spurs in 1999, playing 141 games, scoring 48 goals. However, this would not be Armstrong's last issues with drugs. After retiring from football in 2005, his issues with drugs were highlighted again after a raid on his Kensington home. He was found guilty of possessing cannabis, cocaine and ecstasy. After his arrest he told tabloid newspapers, "I don't have a drug problem".
Unfortunately, this was not his last brush with the law. In 2021, he was charged with assault by beating and criminal damage. This came after causing £2000 worth of damage to his local Tesco and assaulting a shopworker. This was after he was not allowed to buy cigarettes. The reason he gave in court for this was his drink and drug issues had spiralled out of control due to the pandemic. The court were lenient in their sentencing as he avoided jail and was given an 18-month community order. As well as rehabilitation for drugs and alcohol. The FA revealed they have increased funding to the PFA to £24.94 million in 2022-23. This is to be used in part to support former players experiencing mental health and well-being issues. It seems though that Armstrong even after his 2016 conviction has not received the support he may need. At the time of the assault, he was unemployed, with his lawyer saying on top of his drink and drug issues, "He is essentially living month to month at the moment".

The next player to receive a ban was in 2003, when at the time Chelsea's Australian goalkeeper Mark Bosnich was banned. He was banned for nine months for a positive test for cocaine. Bosnich had joined Chelsea from Manchester United where he played a similar role as back-up goalkeeper. This came after almost seven years as Aston Villa's number one playing 179 games. At the time he was regarded by some as one of the best goalkeepers during the 90's. injuries plagued both his time at United and Chelsea however, and this lack of playing time could be the cause of his newfound love of the nightclub scene. Most in the media though blamed this on his relationship with model Sophie Anderton. Anderton at the time was in most newspapers' celebrity gossip columns weekly. It was also known that her party lifestyle had made her a regular cocaine user too.

At the time of his positive test Bosnich strenuously denied he had willingly taken cocaine, saying that the positive test must have been due to his drink being spiked. The FA however didn't believe this, and his appeal was rejected. Sports Minister at the time Richard Caborn was angry with the FA for being too 'lenient'. He believed the FA should've shown support to WADA's request for two-year bans for positive cocaine tests. Chelsea didn't stand by their player either, and sacked the player. This just after Bosnich had entered treatment for depression. Once again, an appeal for unfair dismissal against Chelsea was thrown out by the Premier League who supported the club's decision. Any drug ban doesn't come at a right time, but even worse for Bosnich was that he was close to joining Bolton Wanderers at the time. The FA ensured his ban meant he was banned from football worldwide. At this point Bosnich's life now spiralled out of control. In an interview with a Sunday tabloid newspaper, he said that after his ban he then developed an addiction to cocaine. "I wasn't taking any drugs when I was found guilty by the FA. In 15 years of football, I never touched them. But everybody believed that I was into drugs, especially because of my relationship with Sophie. So, one day I thought, f*** it, I'm going to do it. I went to a club, bought a £50 wrap of coke, and brought it home to try. Basically, I cracked".

This then led to a habit were at his worst, he was doing ten lines a day. He claimed for every line that Anderton did, he had to have one too. He said in 2019 that, "I had given up not only on football but on myself". At this point he became a recluse, the relationship with Anderton broke down, not to the surprise of many. Before his positive test his teammate John Terry had tried to warn him to not become involved with Anderton and her circle of friends. But it was an incident with his father in 2007 that forced him to give up drugs. This was after he nearly shot his father with an air rifle, believing he had an intruder in his home. It was then that his father convinced him to quit. In 2008, he was declared bankrupt at the high court in London. However, his health at this point had improved and so had his fight against addiction. So much so that he had returned to Australia and managed to regain his fitness enough to sign for the Central Coast Mariners. This after the support of his former Chelsea teammate Ed de Goey, who allowed him to train at QPR in 2007, due to his role as a goalkeeping coach. He then finished his career at Sydney Olympic in 2009. He is now a football expert, analyst and commentator for Fox Sports. A role he first started in 2008 for an Australia friendly versus Nigeria. He now lives permanently in Australia and has remained sober. Bosnich realised how fortunate he was in 2019 when he said it was lucky that, "you are talking to me at all". Bosnich had the sport and job he loved so much taken away from him and received no support off Chelsea or the FA. His addiction could've led to his death, except for intervention from family. All this due to a ban from football for a drug that at the time of banning Bosnich the FA clarified, had not been taken to enhance his performance.

Chelsea was once again at the centre of another case involving a failed drug test resulting in a ban. The player in question this time was the Romanian striker, Adrian Mutu. Mutu completed a £16million switch to the Blues from Parma in 2003. He came with a huge reputation for scoring goals, after scoring 18 goals in 31 games in his only season at Parma. The now cash-rich Chelsea who had recently been taken over by Roman Abramovic made him one of their marquee signings that summer. He had a disappointing debut campaign at Stamford Bridge, despite scoring four goals in his first four Premier League appearances under Claudio Ranieri. The Romanian striker only bagged another two for the remainder of the season. Ranieri was replaced at the start of the next campaign by Jose Mourinho. It was reported that Mourinho was trying to offload Mutu that summer after the disappointing first campaign. However, Chelsea found it difficult to find anyone who would purchase him that summer, meaning he would start the campaign at Chelsea.

Only a month into the season though Mutu tested positive for cocaine. This came after he missed a training session after he was excluded from a Champions League squad to play PSG. This was due to a poor performance in a Premier League fixture against Aston Villa the previous week. Due to missing training with 3 other players, he was selected by drug testers. Mutu didn't even give a B-sample to his positive first test, admitting straight away what he had done. He was banned for seven months, which would mean he was not allowed to play until May. He was sacked by Chelsea, just how they had also dealt with Bosnich. But there was big difference, this time Chelsea wanted the money they had spent on Mutu back. They complained to FIFA, who agreed with Chelsea's claim, despite appeals from Mutu. Mutu was extraordinarily ordered to pay back Chelsea the whole £16million fee, they had paid the previous year. Mutu once again put multiple appeals in, but even in 2019, Chelsea is still chasing for the money owed by Mutu. Mutu despite going on to have quite a successful spell in Italy, briefly with Juventus and more successfully with Fiorentina, would never be able to afford this £16million fine. He has lodged his appeals based on Abramovic reportedly having an associate sitting on the panels. But all these appeals have been thrown out and Chelsea still expect the money to be paid. £16million is a large fee for most clubs, however prior to the Russia-Ukraine war, Abramovic wasn't urgently needing the money, he was a multi-billionaire. So, the level of pettiness to keep chasing this money, once again brings into question their treatment of the player.

Mutu we can surmise was using drugs due to how things were going at Chelsea and didn't expect to be tested due to skipping training. When in fact this was the marker that made the drug testers select him. The thing is, instead of keeping him on the books and selling him in the summer to recoup some of the money, there mission to punish Mutu has left them with no return at all. The player's mental health and issues with drugs were once again not addressed, and even more pressure has been put on him since then with the fine hanging over his head for the last 18 years. This would also not be Mutu's last incident of a failed drug test. In 2010, he was banned for nine-months at Fiorentina. This time it was PED's. He tested positive for an appetite suppressant Sibutramine. This was said to come from slimming tablets that had been prescribed to his mum. The silver lining this time that Fiorentina stood by him and didn't fine him for his whole lifesavings. FIFA after deciding the fine, also decided to punish Mutu further by not allowing his name to be used in FIFA computer games for the rest of his career. His name would appear as "Murgu". Hopefully it didn't bother him too much, but I'm presuming he was more concerned about finding £16milliom from somewhere.

The next positive drug test to be released was Jake Livermore. This is a big gap from the previous positive test to be released into the public domain coming in 2015. The reason for the gap in time, was due to how the positive test was found. Livermore tested positive for cocaine, after a game against Crystal Palace, which resulted in a 2-1 for his team Hull City. Once again this is extremely unlucky for Livermore as explained, if the test comes during training, this would never have become public knowledge and he would've been offered a rehabilitation programme. But due to it being in game it's deemed performance enhancing and he would now face the possibility of a 6 month ban or a maximum of up to 2 years.

After the test Livermore was given a provisional suspension by both the FA and his club Hull City, before his case would be heard by an FA panel. The timing couldn't have been worse, Hull were in the middle of a relegation battle from the premier league and Livermore was a key player to their survival. He had become the clubs record signing at the beginning of the season for an undisclosed fee, after helping Hull to reach the FA Cup final the previous year when on loan from Tottenham Hotspur. He was also an England international, although his sole appearance at the time had come in 2012 in a friendly against Italy. Unfortunately, due to the provisional suspension and not having Livermore available, Hull were relegated to the championship at the end of the 2014-15 Premier league season. Steve Bruce explained to the BBC, the reasons that Livermore had turned to the use of cocaine, that summer, as they waited to face the FA panel hearing. "There's no question it was a mitigating factor," Hull manager Steve Bruce told the BBC last month. "Unfortunately, he lost his baby just after the FA Cup final last year. Jake has kept all the problems that he had to himself. All footballers think they are macho men but they have problems like everybody else."

After the high of playing in an FA Cup final albeit it a losing attempt against Arsenal. Livermore's life went spiralling out of control the next day, when his wife went into labour. "To lose a son in a scenario which should have been under control - and was under control at one point - makes it all harder to deal with. It should have been a glorious and happy time for everyone. It was tragic and very difficult to stomach. That is one place I wouldn't want anyone to be." Livermore told former professional Jermaine Jenas the following year in an interview with football focus. Livermore revealed that the fact this come at the end of the season, not allowing him to follow his daily routine of training and seeking help from the club meant it was a lot harder for him to deal with mentally. He also had to be the 'rock' for the rest of his family, as they were affected too and he felt he couldn't seek help, he was helpless. Livermore said he was glad when he was finally found out. "At least people knew the mental state I was in needed addressing," he said. "It was something a lot deeper that I needed to get off my chest. But whether you're too strong to talk about it or not strong enough, it didn't come out."

It was also found after his son's death that the service they received from the hospital in a review of his care. That his death was due to a 'catalogue of errors'. Further fuelling the depression and despair Livermore will have felt, knowing it could have been avoidable. Describing the positive test, as his "get out of jail free card". His manager Steve Bruce at the time felt like he had let Livermore, down not knowing what his player was going through or being able to help him. Livermore blamed nobody else though as he realised he should've just been open with how he was feeling but chose to hide it. His suspensions were later lifted owing to the extenuating circumstances. Livermore praised how his manager, teammates and club owner supported him after his cocaine use come out. He also praised the FA once they found out the reasons for his use. "The FA and Professional Footballers' Association, once it all came out, have been nothing but supportive. That's something I would urge any young player with troubles to do... to go and talk to those people."

It's positive to see that Livermore wasn't punished further than the initial suspension. The FA saw sense as well when considering a ban as the situation Livermore had to deal with is inconceivable for any parent. What is a shame is that his name was released to the press before he was able to explain the reasons for his cocaine use, he should've had the anonymity that players who have tested positive outside of a post-match test receive. Livermore was fortunately able to resurrect his career after this though with the right support. He helped Hull to be promoted back to the premier league the following season, before moving to West Bromwich Albion, who paid £10million for his services, where he remains now. He also went on to play a further 6 times for England in 2017, just missing out on playing at the 2018 World Cup as he was named as a standby.

The next case I feel took onboard the issues of releasing names before the case was reviewed in front of the panel. Allowing the player anonymity until then facing the panel. Which like with a case involving a crime, I feel should happen until the person is proven guilty. The issue in this case was that after finding the person guilty of having cocaine in their system, during testing after a match. The person was then banned for 14-months for the supposed performance enhancing benefits we know aren't true. But worst of all their name was released to the press and the details of the case. Thus, ruining the persons chances of returning to the club they played for prior to the positive test. The reason being the club didn't want to have to deal with the bad press surround supporting a player who had just been banned for the use of cocaine.

They had agreed however if this hadn't come out, like with training ground positive tests and the club not having to release the information, that he would remain their player. Giving him a second chance to redeem himself and continue his dream of being a professional footballer. Instead by the time he got on the train back to Liverpool from his Wembley hearing, the FA had already released the news on their own website and to the press. Not only taking football away for the 14-months they had been banned (6 already served waiting for hearing) but ruining his chances at resurrecting his career at a professional club. The player is the least recognisable of any on the list but is especially poignant for me as it was a close friend from school. I witnessed how this decision made his life spiral out of control, and still to this date, never returned to professional football after this decision was made in May 2017. The player was Paddy Lacey, at the time a 24-year-old midfielder playing for Accrington Stanley in league 2. He made a mistake by taking cocaine, but maybe his bigger mistake was getting caught with it in his system on a match day, rather than at the training ground. He would have received a slap on the wrist, a rehabilitation programme and performance dependent still be a professional to this date.

In the excellent Michael Calvin book, 'No hunger in paradise', which looks at how young players are treated, gives an overview of what young players deal with to become a professional. Children In football clubs at a young age are a statistical anomaly. Less than 0.05% of boys who enter the academy structure at the age of 9 will make a first team appearance. More than 75% are released between the ages of 13 and 16. For those who get past that point don't fare much better. Almost 98% of boys given a scholarship at 16 are no longer in the top 5 domestic leagues at the age of 18. Paddy was faced with these pressures from a young age. His dream like many others was to become a professional footballer, but from a young age entered the academy system at various clubs. He was released at 16 by Blackburn but signed his YTS at Sheffield Wednesday. He was part of the 'lucky' 2% to receive a professional contract from Wednesday before deciding instead to sign with Bradford City. His whole life had focussed to this moment, with it the others who achieve this bring his family and themselves much joy and pride. The sacrifices they make to get there to their bodies and mind, could only be comprehended by those who've achieved the feat. However, his introduction to the professional game, the thing he had worked so far, was disastrous.

Like many other's injuries plagued his first months at the club. Injuries that required surgeries to his knee. He was loaned out to gain experience like many clubs do, and just as he was returning to fitness again, was injured in the last game of his loan spell playing for a non-league team. After only 6 months in the professional game and injured again, he was paid up by the club and released. The decisions for this are wholly situational, Paddy remembers, "The manager had changed to Phil Parkinson and he told me that he liked me. But the club were struggling at the time and for him to bring in his own players, he had to cut the wage budget. Someone like me who was injured and wouldn't cost much to pay up was the easy choice and he took it." After working so hard to achieve his dream it was all over like that. Paddy would then have to start a whole new route to reach the professional ranks again. This time making his way up the non-league ranks in the hope of been seeing by a league 1/2 team who were scouting the lower leagues. It was at this time, playing part-time in the conference north and carpet fitting of a day that he took cocaine for the first time. "I was out with my mates, I'd been offered drugs by them loads of times and my response always was I'm a footballer, I'm not taking that. Then this one night I said that and one of them responded but you're not really. That stuck in my mind, and I thought I'm not. I'm a carpet fitter who plays football on the weekend". The pressure talented footballers must feel to achieve their potential not from just themselves, but their loved ones can lead to a lot of mental health issues. Paddy said that drug taking is rife in non-league as the leagues cannot afford to pay for the drug tests. This might however be a social issue not linked to football at all. It's reported by the government in 2020, that 1 in 5 16–24-year-olds took recreational drugs. Around 9.4% of the population. I don't want to make it seem football is the only reason all these people have taken drugs because that's not the case. However, issues that have arisen in their career may have led to them dabbling in drugs as a release.

After a few non-league clubs, Paddy was promoted to the conference after winning the conference north with barrow. Shortly after this he was then signed by League 2 side Accrington Stanley. Back playing professional football, things were looking up. He then made his full professional debut after a couple of substitute appearances against Portsmouth. He would score the winner in a 1-0 win, that would also see him win Sky Sports League 2 goal of the month. A run of 6 starts at right back as cover for an injured loanee from Bristol City, saw him becoming a regular in the team and rumours of clubs further up the ladder looking at possibly signing him at the end of the season. It then come as a surprise when he was dropped for the next game, for the returning injured player, with at the time no reason given by the manager. The assistant manager even made sure to say he felt this was harsh. This disappointment however would lead him to make a decision that would ultimately cost him his professional football career. That night he went out, drank lots to forget about how upset he was he didn't play, and this led to him then taking cocaine on the night. Waking up the next morning even more down because of the cocaine he then called in sick for training on the Monday. By a stroke of extreme misfortune, he was then called on the Tuesday and begged by the manager to play in that night's fixture away at Hartlepool, as injuries meant he would start.

Against his better judgement but not wanting to let the team down he travelled down to play. At half time in the game as he walked into the changing rooms another player told him the drug testers were at the game to test players. "I just started to drink loads and loads of water to try flush any remaining stuff out my system. When I went out for the second half I could hardly move because my stomach was that full of water. For the whole second half I wasn't even thinking about the game but the potential that I could be randomly selected. At the end of the game, I walked off the pitch and down the tunnel and there the testers called my name Lacey. It's the worst feeling I've ever had in my life, still to this day, my heart just dropped, there was nothing I could do." He confides in a few of the players on the way home who then rang fellow professionals they knew used cocaine to ask how they had fared on tests in the past and how long it took to get out their system. They all replied to it would be fine as 3 days had passed between taking it and the test. A few weeks past with no news and continuing to play. Before he then received the call from his manager John Coleman, "make sure you're sitting down", telling him he had failed the test and he would be suspended immediately. This was his lowest point as he struggled to tell his family what had happened but eventually did and was supported by them.

Then in May he went to the hearing. He had been to see psychologists and explained that he was struggling with his mental health, and this was reported to the FA. But the writing was on the wall as he arrived at Wembley a PFA representative said he thought it would be a 14-month ban. Which was spot on. He was banned for 14-months, he had already served 6 waiting for the decision. Accrington who had paid him throughout the suspension would stick by him if it was kept in-house. This decision was taken away and released to the press the same day. He was sacked by the club begrudgingly, but rightly to protect their image. Once again all because it was in a competition testing, rather than during training. The death of his auntie followed and then at his lowest mental state, attended Glastonbury festival. Where he was arrested and then locked up for 16-months for counterfeit notes and personal drugs on him.

 Accrington stayed in touch, but no support came from the FA. The decision to take away his dreams isn't the reason he was locked up but will have played a factor in his mental state at that time. "The arrest and prison made me the person I am today, I'm not saying it's because of the FA, because I could've felt sorry for myself, but I didn't. I worked hard every day and decided to change my life." Fortunately, his story doesn't end negatively. He now owns his own carpet company and after a promising amateur boxing career during his non-league days is now 6-0 as a professional boxer. He has never played professional football again but has played for various conference north teams. He knows his dream of being a footballer has now been taken away from him. He himself is to blame for this but he could've been given a second chance if FA testing rules were different, or they allowed him anonymity after the decision. But the lessons he has learnt from this he hopes will now guide the way for his two younger brothers Shea (u16 Manchester United and England) and Luis (u18 Barnsley). "They can look at me and learn what not to do. I would never let them go down that path. They're both better footballers than me and they will achieve their dreams." This realisation came too late for Paddy, but the use of recreational drugs in young footballers is a clear issue and how the FA deal with this may need redefining. I believe rehabilitation programmes and anonymity are spot on, but this should also be for positive tests during matches. It's obvious it's not been taken as a performance enhancer, so the differential treatment and the affect this has on someone's life and therefore mental health is outrageous. There was no aftercare for Bosnich, Mutu or Paddy and this is something the FA need to address.

The most famous of all drug bans though in the history of English football was for neither a positive test related to recreational drugs or PED's. On Tuesday 23rd September 2003, a simple mistake or some may argue purposely missed drug test would lead to one of England's star Players and main stay at Centre-Back banned from Euro 2004. Nobody would expect that day when a car carrying two officials from UK sport and an FA representative, for routine drug tests, into Manchester United's Carrington training ground. would lead to the most expensive footballer in the country, with a combined £48million transfer value being banned for 8 months. The player in question as many will know was Rio Ferdinand, one of Manchester United's and the Premier League's best defenders. That day was a routine drug test at the training ground, where players would be selected at random during the morning and then test at the end of their session. Players would much prefer this form of testing. When selected after a 90-minute match, players would prefer to do anything other than sit in a room waiting to urinate. After the physical exertion of playing a football match and then the loss of fluid from this, it can be a long-drawn-out process. Stuart Pearce and Alan Shearer remember that on England duty this could sometime take more than an hour. If what happened that day was in Athletics, Ferdinand would've faced no punishment. Athletics makes a distinction between refusing to give a sample or simply forgetting to keep an appointment. Unfortunately, for Ferdinand he was in breach of rule E26, for the FA there is no difference between missing a test or refusing to take one. This rule carries a maximum two-year suspension. That day Ferdinand was informed before training that he had been selected to give a sample after the session is ended. According to Ferdinand he completely forgot about this appointment by pure forgetfulness and after showering headed to his car to do some shopping in the Trafford Centre. After the realisation dawned on club officials that Ferdinand had left without giving his sample, they tried frantically to contact him, by the time they did, and Ferdinand realised his mistake he rushed back to Carrington as quickly as he could. But by this time the doping control officers had already left and were unable to return to Carrington that day. Meaning that Ferdinand was now in breach of rule E26. Something that I feel is often missed in the context of this story is that Ferdinand did provide a test albeit late.

The earliest the testers could return was Thursday 25th September, where 44 hours after the original test was meant to be conducted, Ferdinand produced a negative test. This has often been left out of the whole Ferdinand saga. With many opposition fans labelling him a 'smack head' and a 'druggie'. By missing the test, he was instantly judged by all those outside of United as being guilty of taking drugs. This is something that has stuck with throughout his career, if you asked most people, they would not be able to tell you of this negative test. But by missing the test that day, the negative test was irrelevant. Some pessimists would say however, that in the period of the missed test and the actual test, any drugs in Ferdinand's system will have had a chance to leave his system. But the period between the original missed test and actual test was not decided by Ferdinand but the testers. But we will never know for certain that day whether it was on purpose that Ferdinand missed the test for the reasons pessimists will subscribe too or for what I personally believe a simple mistake. This idea was supported by many in the club, especially a man we know is very hard to please from his TV persona Roy Keane. In his autobiography 'The Second Half' Keane says this about the incident. "If it had been me, and the doctor had said I had to do a drugs test, I'd have gone and done it. It wasn't something I'd have forgotten. When a doctor says you've got to do a drugs test, it's not an everyday thing. But then, some people are genuinely forgetful." It was not just England who would suffer from his ban but also United. United would end the season 3rd place behind Arsenal and Chelsea. Their worst finish since the premier league began. Keane continued to say. "I don't think I was annoyed at the time, and I don't think the other players were either. But ultimately, the team suffered. I didn't look at Rio and think that he'd been up to no good, or that there was a hidden reason for what had occurred. I think he genuinely forgot. We paid the price. He was a very good player and we missed him, especially in the second half of the season when the crunch games were coming up."

Ferdinand was handed an eight-month ban and fined £50,000 for missing the routine test at the training ground in September 2003 and lost an appeal against the ban. Ferdinand said this to the High-Performance Podcast at the end of his career: "You get tarnished with that brush and I was bitter at first. I hated the FA. I hated all the people at England who were speaking in my face, who smiled at me, but then banned me. I used all of that – hate and bitterness – and I used all of that, reading all of them articles and all of them people saying, 'he's the drug cheat' and he's this and that. 'He's not going to come back the same." Like we've looked at throughout this chapter the player was once again not supported by the FA throughout this ban and was chastised by the media. The affects this had on his mental health will have been very detrimental again and if he didn't have the support of his club but also his own mental strength this could've ended his career at the top level. Although, he would miss 8 months of football in his prime years, he would return to football after the ban and achieve things those doubters would not believe. Instead, he worked harder than ever, determined to prove that he belonged at United. After his ban, he won five Premier League titles, three League Cups and the Champions League. He made his point to all those he blamed for his ban. Ultimately it was Ferdinand's fault due to missing the test, but the handling of the case and the sentence handed by the FA once again brings about many questions.

In his autobiography 'Rio: My Story' Ferdinand said this about the original aftermath of the missed drug test, which came just before England's final qualified for Euro 2004. "The public had no idea I'd missed a test, so I asked the FA to say I was injured, rather than portray me as guilty before I'd had a chance to prove my innocence." Instead, the FA went public that Rio was being excluded for the drugs test and thus was off the English team until further notice, but he was allowed to keep playing for United in the interim. The English players, Manchester United, and Ferdinand were incensed. There was a feeling that Mark Palios, the new head of the FA was making an example out of Rio. Of Palios, Ferdinand said this, "Palios wanted his FA to be an organisation admired around the world as a tough no-nonsense outfit who were not afraid to crack down hard on their own and I felt like he was going to try and use my situation as the perfect example of that approach." Around this time England players nearly went on strike due to the treatment of Ferdinand led by the United contingent in the squad and their voice Gary Neville. But they were talked out of this by Sir Alex Ferguson. Ferguson said this in his biography. "The sentence 'savage and unprecedented' and David Gill said Rio had been made 'a scapegoat'. Gordon Taylor of the PFA called it 'draconian'. We knew he was innocent; we knew he had been careless, and we knew he had been punished too severely." Like has been pointed out throughout this chapter the methods the FA employ were also questioned by Ferguson. "If you admit to being a drug taker, you are rehabilitated. We felt that the player was telling the truth, whereas the system assumed he was not. Nor did we like the fact that information seemed to be leaking to the press from the FA." The positive to come from this whole case is that now players don't have the opportunity to miss tests due to a lapse of memory. In Ferdinand's case the testers were reported to be upstairs drinking tea in the doctor's office. This has now changed so that players are follows straight from the pitch to give tests without the opportunity to leave, much like the testing we see at a match. Ferdinand acknowledges this, "Since my case the drug-testing procedure has changed completely. They've almost got handcuffs on you from the moment your name is picked out at training. You can't go anywhere without a tester following you." This view was shared by Gary Neville in his autobiography 'Red' who said, "Thanks to Rio a shambolic system was overhauled, so at least one good thing came out of it."

This chapter has come in the section of the book winning at all costs. The drugs these players took didn't help them to win, but in most cases were taken to deal with the pressures of staying at the top. Whether that be lower league football or on the biggest stages of football, cocaine in most cases here was a release for the players. They took the drugs when the pressures of being in the public eye was too much or when they weren't achieving the goals, they expected of themselves. The reason the players took these drugs can be directly linked in some ways to the situations they faced due to football the sport they love. Cocaine is a social issue for the whole UK though. The FA believe cocaine is one of the main causes of the increase of disorder in football. They are now imposing 5 year banning orders on fans caught with cocaine on them. A player who wasn't mentioned in this chapter but was no stranger to using cocaine was Paul Merson. Merson was different, he ensured he told his story before anybody else could. He wasn't banned but took part in rehabilitation programmes, like those who are identified prior to matches have and remained anonymous. Merson at his worst missed matches for Arsenal in Europe, saying he had 'tonsilitis' to avoid UEFA mandatory tests. He would go to all-night bars and head straight to training after drinking and snorting cocaine by himself. He would then get a taxi at 8am and would continue to take cocaine on his way to training. His use of cocaine had meant he had hit rock-bottom in terms of his mental health.

He told the Heads-up Campaign after his retirement, "All of that stuff is on you, and you have nobody to talk to. Not a soul. Nobody in the world. All you can do is push it down and down. Going out, you look like Brad Pitt because you're playing for the best team in the country. But of course, it is all masked. You must put a smile on your face." Merson believed players aren't prepared for the fame that comes with football and the pressure, this in term affects their mental health, and drugs is the release for many. Les Ferdinand reflected in the BBC documentary 'The rise of the Premier League', "They have never cared about mental health, you're just a footballer, get on with it." This chapter has outlined this belief of footballers and the lack of thought placed on the care of the players and their mental health.

4
Injuries

"It was very difficult because I went from the highest level in football down to the lowest level of personal unhappiness. It was a very big fall and a really dark time."

Marco Van Basten, three-time Balon D'or winner

The pain in Marco Van Basten's damaged ankle was so severe that by 1994, he would have to crawl from his bed to the bathroom. His only solace and way of diverting his attention from the excruciating pain he felt was to count the time it would take him to reach the toilet. He remembers: "Whispering, I never reach the toilet before I get to 120. The door sills are the most challenging part because my ankle must go over them without touching them. Even the slightest touch makes me bite my lip to prevent a scream." It was only two years earlier that he had won the Balon D'or for a third time and named FIFA's World player of the year. That season would culminate in his final game for AC Milan with who he won three European cups and in the previous season won the scudetto going unbeaten for the whole season. His final game would be the 1993 champions league final against Marseille mentioned in a previous chapter (see match fixing chapter). After missing six months of the season already through issues with his troublesome ankle again, he would come off injured in the defeat to Marseille in the 86th minute. This the result of a hard tackle from behind from match winner Basile Boli, that would once again require surgery on his ankle. The third of his career already on the same ankle. He still had hopes of taking part in the World Cup 1994 for the Dutch National team, but instead would spend two years on the side lines. It was then on 17 August 1995 he admitted defeat in his battle against his injury. Retiring from football and playing his last game at only 28. Van Basten would make an emotional appearance before Milan fans one more time at a home game at the San Siro, which left not only fans devastated but also manager Fabio Capello in tears. Capello said this on Van Basten's retirement, "Marco was the greatest striker I ever coached. His early retirement was a mortal misfortune for him, for football, and for Milan." His issues with his ankle however dated back to his time at Ajax. "I first got injured in December 1986 and it didn't get better. Johan (Cruyff)had a discussion with the doctor who said: 'He has a problem but it's not going to be worse. He can play.' I had a feeling this is not good. I'm in so much pain. Johan said: 'Listen, we make a deal. You don't play all the competitions and some training you can skip. But you must play in Europe. No matter what happens, you must play the final.' That was the deal we made." That year would see him score the winning goal against Lokomotive Leipzig, in the final of the UEFA cup winners cup in 1987. His scoring feats for Ajax was the reason Cruyff felt the need to ensure he played at all costs in Europe.

He would leave that summer after scoring 128 goals in 133 league matches for Ajax. He would move to Milan with his fellow Dutch international Ruud Gullit, but although Milan would win their first Scuddeto in eight years, would see Van Basten only play 11 games due to his ankle. The following year would see Van Basten at his peak though as he recovered to score 32 goals in all competitions as he won the European cup with Milan and Euro 1988 with Holland, scoring the spectacular volley remembered by all in the final against the Soviet Union, whilst scoring 5 goals at the tournament. Had Van Basten taken a break instead of continuing to play in 1987 at the request of his hero Johan Cruyff, would he have avoided the issues that caused him to retire? In an interview with The Guardian in 2020 he said this, "In the beginning the doctors didn't give me good advice. I went on and on and the damage got worse. The next season I went to Milan with Gullit. I played the first few matches in August-September, then I went to another doctor in Barcelona, and we made the decision to have an operation. It was too late, because the damage was done." As his career continued although to most, he was still one of the best in the world, evidenced by his Balon D'or wins in 1988, 89 and 92, the pain in his ankle became too much and his future way of life took precedent over his football career. "After a lot of problems with operations I was limping. I couldn't do anything without pain. I was really handicapped, and the doctors couldn't help me. I was a little afraid. It had gone from bad to worse. After many operations, and seeing doctors from all over the world, I had tried everything, but we couldn't find the solution. There was a moment in 1996 I had to say: 'I have to try to get healthy.' We decided to fuse my ankle. For a sportsman, and I was still only 32, that's the worst choice. But I had to stop the pain."

Even at 56 Van Basten was still limited in what he could do now, showing the tolls football takes on players bodies long term and what they put themselves through for the sport they love. "I don't have any pain, but I am limited. I can't play tennis or football. But I play squash and I am thankful. Looking back, I was feeling it was a pity I couldn't finish my career after winning more Champions League [titles]. I wanted to show more of myself. Some players have 18 years in football. But some players are injured before they start. When I thought like that I said: 'If I compare with that, I have been very lucky. At least I had 10 years of a beautiful experience that changed my life for ever.'"

Van Basten despite playing his last game at 28 was ranked sixth in the FIFA player of the century internet poll. He was also ranked by Sky Sports in 2007, first on their list of great athletes who had their careers cut short. This probably not an award Van Basten longed to achieve, but this chapter will set out to look at some examples from English football of players who have had their career cut short by injury, ruining their dreams of playing the sport they loved at the very top for as long as possible. Something that we all know from playing football and any sport can sometimes not be avoided. However, this chapter will look at others who like Van Basten felt pressured to play despite the long-term effects it had not only on their career but their health and mental health. Whilst others did it for fear of losing their place in teams to positional rivals and combated this with the use of painkillers to numb their pain. Painkillers that would then cause them as many issues as their injuries had already done previously if not worse. All this though to continue to play the sport they love, that would leave some unable to do the simplest of physical tasks; due to the permanent damage of an accidental injury during games or training, but in some cases due to tackles with malice bore out of anger towards them.

If you ask anyone of a tackle that left one player permanently damaged, due to a 'premeditated' tackle from an opponent, the first one people think of is Roy Keane on Alfe-Inge Haaland. Keane revealed in his 2002 autobiography exactly what was said during a notorious incident. He wrote: "I'd waited long enough. I f*cking hit him hard. The ball was there (I think). Take that you c***. And don't ever stand over me sneering about fake injuries." If you haven't seen the tackle (which I doubt many won't have not seen), it is a shocking knee-high tackle in the last few minutes of the Manchester derby in 2001. Even after seeing his opponent stricken on the floor Keane stood over Haaland hurling verbal abuse at his opponent. The reason for this vicious tackle and the continued abused, dated back to an incident four years previously in 1997. During a Premier League clash with Leeds at Elland Road, Keane ruptured is ACL. This came after a coming together with Haaland, who had recently signed for Leeds from Nottingham Forest. Many in the crowd and Haaland himself didn't believe that Keane was in as much pain as he was, leaving Haaland to be seen shouting at Keane on the floor, much like he would be reciprocated to him four-years later.

The injury would cause Keane to miss most of the 1997-1998 campaign and go through his own battle with a serious injury. This injury and the time out of the sport Keane loved, added to Haaland's reaction towards him, would cause Keane to never forgive or forget the incident. In an interview with GiveMeSport in 2022, after his son Erling signed for Manchester city said this about the initial incident. "He tried to tackle me, and I got the free kick. He was lying on the ground, and I just told him to 'get up' as you normally do with players – nothing more than that. I wasn't trying to intend anything against him, but obviously he took that very hard." In 2002 Keane revealed the notorious comments above in his autobiography regarding the incident. After the original incident, Keane was fined £5,000 at the time and given a three-match suspension, but comments in his book saw him stung for a further £150,000 while also being ruled out of another five matches.

Even in 2014 though Keane would double down on his original comments in his newly released autobiography 'The Second Half'. "[He] p*ssed me off, shooting his mouth off. He was an absolute pr*ck to play against. Niggling, sneaky.I did want to nail him and let him know what was happening. I wanted to hurt him and stand over him and go: 'Take that, you c***.'I don't regret that. But I had no wish to injure him. It was action; it was football. It was dog eats dog. I've kicked lots of players and I know the difference between hurting somebody and injuring somebody. I didn't go to injure Haaland. When you play sport, you know how to injure somebody. There was no premeditation. I'd played against Haaland three or four times between the game against Leeds, in 1997, when I injured my cruciate and the game when I tackled him, in 2001, when he was playing for Manchester City. If I'd been this madman out for revenge, why would I have waited years for an opportunity to injure him? Was I going around for years thinking: 'I'm going to get him; I'm going to get him.'? No. Was he at the back of my mind? Of course, he was."

It has now become common folklore in football that Keane ended Haaland's career which is a point of contention for Keane as well. "Haaland finished the game and played four days later, for Norway. A couple of years later he tried to claim that he'd had to retire because of the tackle. He was going to sue me. It was a bad tackle, but he was still able to play four days later." This is true that Haaland did finish the game and played for Norway four days later, as well as playing 68 minutes in City's next league fixture. Haaland did undergo surgery that summer, in what was to be the beginning of the end for him, but that operation was carried out on his left leg, while Keane clattered into his right.

Even Haaland, has admitted that the former United captain cannot shoulder sole responsibility for him having to cut short a career in England, in his 2022 interview he said, "I don't blame him. I never actually said he finished my career. It was my last full game in England, so maybe he had something to do with it." He also told BBC Sport in 2014 of his clashes with Keane: "I don't blame him for kicking me in other games or that game. What I was concerned and worried about is that he said, in his first book, that he wanted to take revenge. And I don't think that's part and parcel of football." So, what had stemmed from one player's inner turmoil at their own serious injury and the reaction of their opponent, caused him to seek revenge in some way against that opponent and although not being the ultimate factor that would cause Haaland to retire, played some part in his mind. Haaland would retire in 2003 never playing a full game for City again at the age of 31 but has had some comfort in seeing the success of his son now becoming one of the most feared strikers in the world. Haaland though will still be left to question that tackle and its potentially repercussions on his career. "For eight years, I wasn't injured. Coincidence or not, that was my last 90 minutes in England. Is that a coincidence, or isn't it? I haven't played a full 90 minutes after that incident, that's the fact. And people can judge whatever they want".

The next incident also saw a terrible tackle, however this time the player dishing out the tackle ended up causing more harm to themselves. It was a miracle that only one player came out of that tackle seriously injured and anybody watching the tackle would not believe the player on the receiving end would be the one coming off relatively unscathed. The player injured was Paul Gascoigne in the FA cup final at Wembley. Gascoigne playing for Spurs had scored a 30-yard free kick in the semi-final to see them past their north London rival's arsenal now. At the time he was one of the hottest properties in Europe and was set to join Lazio that summer in 1990.

However, his tackle on Forest player Gary Charles would see his game end after ten minutes. In today's game it wouldn't have just ended for him due to his injury but a red card. Possibly more shocking was the fact he had got away with a similar horror tackle only minutes before, the occasion clearly getting to him. "I remember Charles coming down the right," he recalls. "His touch brought him inside and I was off balance. I tried to get a good

96

challenge on him to let him know he was in a game." It wasn't a good challenge - for Spurs or Gascoigne. It gave Forest the free kick that Stuart Pearce would convert to give them the lead. And it meant a premature end to what should have been a momentous day for Gascoigne in his last game as a Tottenham player. "I got up and knew I wasn't feeling right," says Gascoigne. "I got back in the wall and Pearce scored but I wasn't bothered about that. All I was thinking about was my injury." Straight after the restart he would fall to the floor and his game was over and he now faced a lengthy spell on the side-lines. Tottenham's physio John Sheridan remembers this about the whole situation in his autobiography 'The Limping Physio: A life in Football''. Sheridan said: "Paul tried to play on at first, then I ran on to the pitch the second time and we both knew it was a serious injury straight away. I remember after he came off, waiting for the doctor and we both had tears in our eyes. I went to the hospital the next morning, got up at 6.30am, I was in the operating theatre and watched the surgery. I remember at the time that there was a fear that he would not play at the top level again. There was so much pressure at the time. Tottenham's finances meant they were counting on the transfer, and it was a huge deal at the time. The pressure on me was huge. Lazio gave him a deadline to get fit."

Luckily for Spurs Lazio didn't pull out of the £5.5million move and waited for Gascoigne to return to fitness before buying him the following summer. Some believe that he didn't reach the same heights during his three seasons in Rome but is still revered by the Lazio fans. Many believe the injury never just stole Gascoigne of his dream of lifting the FA Cup in person and not just watching from a hospital bed, but affected the rest of his playing career, never being quite the same again. This is something that angers Sheridan. "People ask whether he was still the same player afterwards or if he would have been a better player but for that injury," said Sheridan. "But he played more games for England after that injury than before, and would a fully fit player been able to score that goal against Scotland in Euro 96? Looking back, I'm incredibly proud of what we achieved." The injury still haunts Gascoigne to this day and mixed with a lot of complex issues in his past is another lasting memory that upsets him to this day. "The minute I started crying was the minute they started walking up the steps," he says. "That was my dream. I still get a lump in my throat when I talk about it. I wasn't bothered with lifting the trophy, I just wanted to walk up those steps."

A mail on Sunday report laid bare the pressures on young players. It emerged that almost 2,500 players have sought professional help with their mental health since 2018 alone. A total of 2,434 professional footballers in the UK accepted the PFA's offer to provide them with therapeutic support in the past four and half years. The reasons given for this are to deal with the emotional rollercoaster of football and the industry hazards, one being long-term injury. Others include finances and family issues (being away from family and breakdown of relationships) all related to football and the pressures of football. That's been the highest uptake, in the use of this support, which although it highlights how delicate players mental health has become, is also a positive that players are seeking help for this, where there may have been a stigma attached to this previously. The PFA offer players emotional support through their wellbeing department, which is run by director of player welfare Dr Michael Bennett, a former professional with Wimbledon and Charlton. Like most of those in this chapter, he also struggled with the expectations of a footballer, before then suffering a serious knee injury himself, that nearly derailed his career.

'I want players to know that there is support available to them now, that was not there when I was a player,' he said. A proposal has been made by a leading coach of one of the top six Premier League clubs, who spoke to Sports Mail on the promise of anonymity, that they believe FIFA should bring in new rules to force footballers to rest between matches to stop players putting their physical and mental health at risk. The coach admitted that "we're playing with players' health. i newspaper has also investigated this, and the risks players put themselves at. The body hurts for most players from the start of preseason starting with something minuscule like blisters from new boots. Then your feet and ankles start to hurt as preseason fully kicks in. Then your whole-body aches due to the relentless schedule of matches that players face, with every part of the body feeling the overload of playing football. Playing in pain is what is expected of players and for a player to succeed at the highest level, players are expected to come to terms with this. But at what cost to the players?

In their investigation 'i' uncovered that coaches at the highest level had grown increasingly worried with the culture of players masking pain and injury. Clubs disregarding the welfare of their players as they pushed their bodies to the limit as they pursued trophies and glory. What also concerned them was that players are displaying signs of addiction to the drugs they are taking to block out the pain they feel. The drugs they're taking are legal, but they can be potentially serious in damaging their physical and mental health. One such player is former England and Spurs defender Danny rose who believes the cortisone and platelet-rich plasma injections he had administered while recovering from a knee injury triggered his depression. The investigation also found that others are masking broken bones, and some believe that abusing painkillers prematurely ended their careers. Jason Roberts, who played as a professional for two decades before retiring in 2014 though injury said this regarding pain relief. "I've seen players get to a point where pain relief becomes part of the routine," he says. "I've always done it: I did it Tuesday, I had a good game I'll do it Thursday; I did it Thursday, had a good game, and so on. That is something that possibly needs to be looked at." Roberts once played on for an hour with a hairline fracture in his right leg. The 40-year-old will require two hip operations and has been advised not to run again. He has metal rods in several parts of his body. "My body hurts, I'm in pain all the time," he says, "and I was lucky with injury, there are guys in much worse states than me."

A player who felt his career was cut short due to the misuse of painkillers was former Liverpool defender Daniel Agger. Agger retired in 2016 and was another player who was unfortunately tagged with the injury prone tag. He struggled constantly through his career with a prolapsed disc in his back and told Danish newspaper Jyllands-Posten. "The body could not cope with it," he said. "I have taken too many anti-inflammatories in my career. It could be that others take a pill or two less." The opinion that using painkillers to allow players to play at all costs is not supported by all managers. This was a point of contention during Pep Guardiola's time in Bayern Munich, where he clashed with club doctor Hans-Wilhelm Muller-Wohlfahrt. "He completely neglected the medical profession," Muller-Wohlfhart told German broadcaster ZDF. "It was not about recovery of the players, but only freedom from pain. It was not about the healing of injuries; it was completely against my philosophy." During the time he was at Munich the club doctor was regularly questioned about the recovery time of players and felt players were often rushed back to play, or to use painkillers to play no matter their injuries.

A player who knows all about the risks of painkillers and unlike others has come out and spoke about how his misuse of painkillers led to his life spiralling out of control is Goalkeeper Chris Kirkland. During the worst period of this suicide had crossed his mind, as his mental health deteriorated. "What happened to Gary Speed was the thing that really worried me," Kirkland says, with reference to the Wales midfielder's death in 2011. "I didn't know how far away I was from that. Hopefully, a long, long way. I always ask myself: 'Would I have done something to myself? Would I have harmed myself? I like to think I wouldn't have done. I certainly didn't sit there one night, thinking, right, I've got to … you know. But you think about it. You do, yeah. Because you don't want to wake up. I said to my wife, Leeona, that I couldn't wait to go to sleep at night and just be clear. But then, I didn't want to wake up in the morning because it just starts again. I'd never have done it because of Leeona and our daughter, Lucy. But I was worried how close I was to the next step. That's why I said: 'I need to stop playing football." During the start of his career at Liverpool and a loan spell at West Brom he suffered from injuries, but what annoyed him was the fact this stuck with him for the rest of his career as people labelled him injury prone. This despite the fact his injury record post 2006 being excellent. "That's one of the things that has griped at me – that people say I was always injured, when I wasn't," Kirkland says.

During Liverpool's 2005 Champions League winning campaign, Kirkland played 4 group matches before injury ruled him out for the rest of the season. The what if's of whether he stayed fit in his time at Liverpool are what he regrets most in his career. "I always wonder, and I can't help it, where I would have got to if I had been injury-free," he says. "My career could have been a lot better. When people say Chris Kirkland, they say: 'Always injured.' It's not like: 'Chris Kirkland; he won the Champions League.' Like the top players. That's just another factor that has piled up." Due to his 4 appearances, he did win a Champions League winners medal but was only in the stands with his wife to watch the game and then also wasn't allowed on the team flight home that meant he was unable to be part of the victory parade. After leaving Wigan he joined Sheffield Wednesday, and it was here that his battle with painkiller misuse began and took over his life. Kirkland felt he was flying during pre-season at Wednesday after two difficult final seasons at Wigan Athletic, where he lost his place, but two days before the opening game of the Championship campaign he sustained a back injury. "I thought: 'Fuck, if I don't play on Saturday, I'm going to get crucified.' Everyone's going to say: 'Told you so.' In the contract there was a clause that if I missed three games with a back injury, they could rip the deal up. At the start of the season there is that Saturday-Tuesday-Saturday, so within a week I could be gone. That was playing on my mind, so I got hold of some painkillers, tramadol, [which] took the pain away and helped me with the anxiety of travelling away from home, to and from Sheffield. You're not meant to take any more than 400mg a day of tramadol and I was on 2,500mg a day," he says, "In the end they don't work, they just mess you up, mentally. You kid yourself thinking: 'I'll stop next week; I'll stop next week.' I had a couple of bad incidents where I took 10 or 12 of them, so over 2,000mg, and I was hallucinating in the house. I had heart palpitations, was in and out of consciousness. That made me stop for a few days because I thought: 'I'm going to kill myself here.' But then the addiction kicks in, your body craves it, you get the aches and pains, and you know that if you take them, they'll go away. I didn't want to speak to people, and it made it very difficult for Leeona and Lucy in the house. Without them I wouldn't be here, simple as that."

So how did Kirkland manage to overcome his addiction to painkillers and survive his battle with his mental health too. "The postman knows not to give me any letters or parcels," Kirkland says, "because I was buying them off the internet. Now he knows never to give me anything, so it always goes to Leeona. We've put things in place to hopefully prevent it from happening again.". Leeona, who he refers to as a saint and an angel, drug tests him every couple of days. "I'm due one, actually," he says. "If you are struggling with any kind of addiction, you can't do it yourself; it's impossible. You'll be kidding yourself. Be brave, ask for help and the quicker you get it, the better you'll be." Has not taking them meant his back pain has worsened? "It's probably better. The painkillers will say: 'You're really sore, really sore, take me and you'll be fine' and, upstairs, that is what it does to you. I would love to play golf every day, but I can't, because it would be agony. I can't do road runs because of the pounding, but I can walk. I can go out on the bike. I can't lift weights. I know exactly what I can and can't do." Even through all the pain and how much it has affected his life, Kirkland still says this, "I'd do it all again for just one game for Liverpool, that's how much the club means to me."

Another player who knows of the risk of painkillers is Ryan Cresswell, who like Kirkland is rare that he has openly discussed the risks of painkillers. Cresswell started at Sheffield United, before playing his career outside of the English top-flight. He said: 'I think there is a big issue in football with sleeping tablets and I mean from the top, as high as you can go. 'For me it started with one after every game, which was great, and I think is an alright purpose to use them. But then it went from one after games, to one a day to two a day and then I knew I was addicted to them. It was not me craving it, it was my body, I knew it wasn't the right thing. It's horrible. There will be 22 or 23-year-old lads now in the Premier League, Championship, wherever taking too many painkillers. It will not be for another three years that they realise they have a real problem. The sweats and the shakes at night will come and they just must get through it.' Cresswell has recently achieved a year sober, but only after his second spell at the sporting chance clinic.

His toughest times came as he took painkillers to treat a chronic knee injury during his time at Northampton, which led to him having to attend rehab and suffering a relapse. Even though he is now in a better place. He still must attend alcoholic anonymous meetings to, to deal with issues he suffers from alcohol misuse that he mixed with his painkiller and sleeping tablet misuse. "Painkillers, sleeping tablets and drink. I was way out of my depth. I can't believe I did what I did. When I went into rehab for the first time, I thought I hit a low, but I hadn't even dived in the pool. When I went in the second time I was gripping on for dear life. It was a matter of life or death. I didn't want to die. Some people have passing thoughts about not wanting to be here anymore, I was living in those thoughts. I'd been in the depths of despair for a few months and this one morning I'd decided enough was enough and that I couldn't do it anymore, I was thinking, 'I'm hurting the people around me, I'm a s**** dad, I'm a s*** husband'. I was completely gone, reality had hit in. I felt like I was going to jump in front of a train." Luckily his second spell in rehab has managed to allow him to see a light at the end of the tunnel. But once again shows the risk of playing through pain and masking it with painkillers. There is probably plenty of other players who have dealt with the same issues, and it is something that hasn't been spoken about enough. Players feel pressured to be on the pitch and this is causing them to risk their own health at times.

From watching football my whole life, I feel as though strikers are the worst affected by injuries. Obviously, any form of leg break or cruciate ligament damage is going to cause serious problems for

104

any player. But with some strikers, you feel as though when they lost that yard of pace, they had over most it put them at a serious disadvantage. Some are unfairly labelled as only being speed merchants, when that's not true, as nobody has ever made it as a footballer professionally just because they're fast. Look at what happened when Usain Bolt attempted to become a professional footballer. Pace and nothing else may make a perfect Sunday league player, whose team lump balls over much slower defenders, but at the top level this isn't possible. However, although much more to some forwards, that yard of pace is what made them standout against the rest and a nightmare for any defender. Losing this pace makes players must adjust the way they play and for some means they are not as effective as they have been in their early years prior to injury.

Watching Liverpool, I have been privileged to watch some of the best strikers in the Premier League at certain periods. Michael Owen, being one of those. Although he may not be remembered fondly by all Liverpool fans now after the manner of his exit and then consequent signing for Manchester United many years after, there is no arguing with how devastatingly good he was for Liverpool.

He was the last English recipient of the Balon D'or, winning it at only 21, as well as being Liverpool's top goal scorer every season between 1997-2004. Owen had electric pace, which at times made him impossible to stop, an example of this being the FA cup final in 2001, where he glided past arsenals hapless defenders to score two goals to give Liverpool a win in a game they had been totally dominated. Owen was also a supreme finisher and was not all pace, however hamstring injuries would hamper him from a young age, and without this pace to get himself in positions ahead of defenders, found it difficult to put his excellent finishing to use as much as he had previously. "At 21? Oh, I thought I could win another Balon d'Or,' he says, belief in his young self an unwavering characteristic. 'I still didn't know injuries would compromise me so much. But looking back, even then, I was terrified to run at top speed. From 10 to 17, I believe there wasn't anyone in the world as good. By 18, I was scoring goals at a World Cup. By 21, the Balon d'Or. But honestly, I was better at 19. That was when I suffered a crippling injury. Everything comes back to that." The injury Owen talks about took place in April 1999. In a game against Leeds at Elland Road, Owen ruptured his hamstring. Hamstring injuries would then become a recurring theme of his career, and with damage to his hamstring also came other muscle injuries too. "I wish it had been a broken leg. The worst injury for me was a snapped hamstring, because back then you didn't operate, you just allowed them to reattach. I was running with two hamstring muscles in my right leg and three in my left for the rest of my career. It was a point of weakness." Very similar to Owen in terms of their electric pace and composed finishing was Fernando Torres. Although bigger and stronger than Owen, pace again was the thing that made him feared by most defenders. The similarities for both didn't end there though, as Torres himself also suffered numerous muscle injuries as well as damage to his hamstrings. With that pace gone Torres also struggled to find his clinical form of previous years, one that had saw him score the winning goal for Spain in Euro 2008, where his pace saw him cruise past Philip Lahm before lifting the ball over the onrushing goalkeeper into the goal.

By the time the full effects of injuries had succumbed Torres was on the move to Chelsea, where he was never able to reach the same heights again. But for me, the one player I question how far they could've gone, if injuries hadn't taken their toll was Daniel Sturridge, maybe because he didn't leave Liverpool, like the other two. I would find it very difficult to pick out of all 3 who was the best striker as they were all exceptional. But Sturridge I felt had skill to go with the pace and finishing the other two also possessed. Sturridge however struggled with injuries more frequently than many footballers I can remember (bar Naby Keita, who hands down owns the award for this), and this often-left fans and even his manager questioning him. Klopp said this in 2015, "what is serious pain and what is only pain". This I felt at the time was quite harsh and even when writing this book and above I've just jibed at Naby Keita, it is often unfair to do this to players.

I highly doubt any player doesn't want to play football, if they didn't then why would they have dedicated their whole life to it. I don't also go with the argument that they're earning 'x amount' so why would they care. Well, that's an easy answer, if you don't play and impress this could be your last contract. This is often what causes players to play through the pain barrier, to ensure they don't get a reputation, one that could cause them to no longer be at the top level of football or achieve goals they set out for themselves at the start of their career. Former Wigan and Blackburn forward Jason Roberts discussed this. "From a player's perspective you never want to show any weakness to anyone, ever," Roberts says. "Never want to show a weakness to the manager because then he might drop you next week. You get a reputation. Daniel Sturridge: a reputation as someone who can't play through pain. The narrative is one of a lack of character. That's where it becomes a problem. We're still in a sport and this sport is about winning and losing," Roberts adds. "Often, it's couched in a lack of commitment. And, not just players: by fans, managers, the whole environment sees you as a weak character, if the perception is you can't play through pain. You don't show weakness to anyone, ever. That's the rule. So, if you can play through it you do. "It has been perceived by many and will unfortunately stick with Sturridge for the rest of his career that he is a weak character, and it is this and not the injuries that have stopped him from reaching his full potential many believe he didn't reach.

During a wide-ranging interview with The Independent's Melissa Reddy on her Behind The Lines podcast, Sturridge said: "I saw a quote from Reus the other day saying he'd pay any amount of money to just play injury-free or never be injured. And honestly, I'd do the same. I would pay any amount of money. I already spend loads of money outside of the physios at work to do extra stuff to ensure that I can be as healthy as possible." Sturridge however was still tormented by injuries no matter what he tried to do, to prevent them. "Hundreds of thousands, to be fair, you know, to make sure that my body can be in the best shape possible. And sometimes, you can put the hours in, you can do everything, but… it is just bad luck. The toughest thing is just the mental side because you know you've given your all, you know you slept well, you know you ate well. You know you've got the treatment that you need to get everything right. You've done everything. No one percent is left so when you go through an injury, the mental side of it is very tough - it can continue to break you and send you down a dark path. I've been someone who has played on with injuries, putting my body on the line for the team on countless occasions. I go through the hard things to push myself for the team. I've always done that." From this interview you can see how hurtful these comments not only from his manager, but most football fans could be, as he has put his body on the line to try to help his team win at all costs, even if it was to the detriment of his own fitness.

Unlike in the case of Keane and Haaland, where you could say that it may be down to intent rather than bad luck. That can't be said for many players who unfortunately just get unlucky. Like I believe in Sturridge's case. However, Sturridge still plays in some capacity now in Australia, although his time there has been plagued by injuries too. The other forwards I'm going to discuss now though weren't as lucky, and their injuries cut their careers short and led them to the pits of despair, with football no longer part of their lives.

The first of these players to have their careers cut short due to injury was once described by Brazilian Ronaldo as his favourite strike partner he played with. Ronaldo himself was like Owen and Torres in the fact that injuries took away his pace that made defenders fear him most. But still in my mind is one of the best strikers of all-time even if periods of his career were paused due to injury. When he was fully fit and prior to the injuries that made his game change, he was unstoppable. The player he described as his best strike partner was the Belgian forward Luc Nilis, who when his career ended due to injury, was playing for Aston Villa, after recently signing from PSV Eindhoven. Ronaldo, his former strike partner at PSV, described the Belgian as the best he played with. "I've played with big players like Figo, Romario, Zidane, Rivaldo, Djorkaeff and Raul, but it clicked best with Nilis, with whom I played at PSV," Ronaldo once remarked. Nilis joined Villa after they had reached the FA Cup final the previous year. He came with a sublime reputation, after scoring 266 club career goals prior to joining Villa.

He was not just a great goal scorer though, but a two-footed player also remembered for scoring stunning goals too. It was not just Villa fans excited to see their new signing, but also the whole league, to see whether he could live up to the reputation he had built for himself. In his first league match he showed Villa fans what they could expect and that his reputation hadn't preceded himself, when he scored a stunning goal against Chelsea in his first match at Villa Park. However just two games later, his whole life would be turned upside down, and his football career would be over due to an injury at Ipswich Town. In the game he would collide with goalkeeper Richard Wright and suffer a double fracture of his shin. Complications after the injury would cause him to nearly have his right leg amputated. The whole thing would cause Nilis years of hurt and change his life forever. In an interview with the Athletic many years later, Nilis opened up about how his life changed for the worst. "I was in a dark place, a deep black hole", Luc Nilis says, "It was trauma. Some days, simply getting out of bed would be a struggle." The joys of three young children couldn't even make him smile and his marriage had fallen apart. "It was not a messy split, but, yes, it came as a follow-up from the mental rollercoaster I had been on. When football was taken away from me, I missed it so much that I fell into the black gap. It was mental torture. Every day for a very long time."

"After the operation there were lots of complications," he explains. "There was no blood circulation in my leg, so I almost lost it. I was very scared. In the end they had to operate again because my leg was dying. They had to make two big gaps to get my leg to bleed again so the circulation could start. "After the (second) operation the doctor told me how close I was to losing my leg. It was hard to take in. Eventually, they would slowly close the gaps, day by day, but the damage was done." He sought four independent medical reports, in the months after the injury, and all of them gave the same damning verdict: his days as a professional footballer were over. The damage in his right leg was too much and Villa would therefore cover the cost of the insurance premium, but this didn't provide any rest-bite from the mental effects of the injury and his untimely retirement. "Having to sign the papers (in January 2001) to say I couldn't play football anymore was devastating," he says. "It was the blackest day in my life. I felt like I was born with the football in my bed, then in one second, I must sign that I could never play again. Mentally it was very hard to get over this." Without football Nilis continued to struggle and nothing could fill the void that football now left in his life, the only thing Nilis had ever wanted to do and dreamed of. "My physiotherapist was probably the man who saved me," he says. "He told me that I must get out of bed every morning to visit him otherwise I will end up living like somebody with one leg for the rest of my life. He not only helped me walk again, but also get my life back on track. He said that for every day I don't get out of bed, he will be there to pick me up. I cannot live without football," he says. "It's my life. I lost my life after that injury, but I have picked it back up. I have found a good new spirit." The next three players all suffered the same fate as Nilis, but what also linked them is that before their injury many tipped them to be future stars for England prior to their injuries. The one many felt had the best chance out of the three of becoming a main stay for England upfront was Dean Ashton.

It was on England duty that Ashton would suffer the injury that would subsequently cause his early retirement from football. During a training session in 2006 he broke his ankle due to a tackle from a teammate, at the time nobody could predict how serious the injury would be, but it would cause him to retire 3 years later at 26. This came after his surgeon warned him, he could be left unable to walk if he continued to play. He did return to play almost a full campaign with West Ham the following year, including making his sole England appearance in a June 2006 friendly against Trinidad and Tobago. But a recurrence of the injury after five appearances at the start of the 2008/09 season left him side-lined again, and it was then after consultation with his surgeon that he decided to retire from football in December. His last game prior to the original injury was the FA Cup final against Liverpool, where he showed why he was so highly thought of as he scored and almost led West Ham to victory before they were defeated on penalties. This game Ashton described as his 'best ever'. "As a player, you refuse to entertain the prospect of retiring. You won't let the thought cross your mind," said the former Crewe and Norwich striker. "I was thinking, 'I might be able to have injections, there will be a way to keep going' but it came to the point where there was a very real prospect that I might not be able to walk properly again. I couldn't walk a golf course, or even go out to the shops — suddenly I had to think about my quality of life and my kids, not just about football."

"There's not a day that goes by where I don't think about still wanting to play and what ifs,' he told *Sportsmail*. 'I never got to get to the end of my career and think I've given it everything. I'll always have that. I've always got a reminder with my leg too. My life's never going to be the same, not only in terms of football but also what I can do in my day-to-day life. That's always a reminder. Everyone I ever speak to that loves football wants to talk about what happened and how sad it was. You never forget it. "I didn't watch football for about two years because I was too bitter and twisted to. 'It's torturous. You are known as Dean the footballer; you are not known as Dean the normal person who loves football, and this is his job. That's what you're seen as If you can't do that, you feel pressure from family and friends who come and support you all the time, from the club because they're paying your wages, have maybe put a huge transfer fee on you, from the players, especially if you're a key part of the squad and the team isn't doing well. You feel very inferior and that shouldn't be the case — it is effectively a job and something you enjoy doing, and if you can't do it, that's what's really difficult.'

Ashton talks about in the same interview, how he wishes he would've worked with a psychologist from the start of his career. As when he was at Norwich, he saw this as a bit of a joke and didn't use it to its full advantage. "It was seen as a weakness and you wouldn't want to show any weakness, certainly to the coaching staff because you wanted to play every week. Looking back, in hindsight, I probably should have spoken to a psychologist a bit more frequently. That could have at least helped me.' Something that he now believes is changing for the better and being embraced more by players and clubs. He is concerned about what plans players have though after football and knows from his own experience how football can be taken away from you in the blink of an eye. "For me to turn around and say do your studies and make sure you look after yourself financially, it is difficult for players to take it on board because all they think about is next Saturday. Not what might happen in two weeks if you were to break your ankle and your career is ended next year. You just can't think about it that way. You should, but you don't. It takes such a focus to even make it; people don't dare to think about what could happen." For Ashton his early retirement from football still lingers on his mind every day. "There's not a day that goes by where I don't wish I could still play. I absolutely love it. If I said to anybody that if tomorrow, they could never do the thing they love the most, that is just hard."

Another player like Ashton, who some believe could've been set to become a future England star was Blackburn's Matt Jansen. The 2001/2 Premier League season saw him secure a successful 16-goal haul. This led many to believe he would be included in the World Cup 2002 squad, a view supported by the player himself. Not due to unwarranted self-belief but due to the fact this is what had been relayed to him by his manager Graeme Souness before the squad announcement. "I was told I was going to the World Cup. The team was going to be announced the day after the penultimate game of the season. We were playing Liverpool and Sven [Goran Eriksson] told Graeme Souness, who was Blackburn manager, not to tell me but say "don't get injured" because I was going to be named in the World Cup squad." Jansen came through the match unscathed, and the next day waited round the training ground after a warm-down to hear the squad be announced.

Jansen was also being linked Manchester United, Arsenal and Italian side Juventus. All who supposedly had shown an interest. As he continued to wait around Jansen then became wary that Eriksson had gone back on his word to Souness, something that was confirmed by his agent and brother-in-law. "I rang my brother-in-law, who was my agent at the time, and it transpired that they ended up taking Martin Keown instead. He never played a minute of the World Cup. I had been told I was going. I got my invitation to the David Beckham pre-launch party, I got measured for my suit, I was proud as punch and then I don't get to go at the 11th hour." This was a bitter pill to swallow as Jansen described how he felt before the announcement, "To win the League Cup and get called up by England, my ego was as big as it has ever been. I was at the top of my game, getting more and more confident." Jansen was also not named as a reserve for the tournament with only Danny Murphy occupying this role. He therefore decided to go on holiday to Rome with his girlfriend Lucy. It was on this holiday that he would suffer an injury that he believes led to his career being cut short. He was driving a scooter with Lucy on the back when they were knocked over by a taxi, which led to head injuries that caused Jansen to be placed in a coma for 6 days. "We were coming around a corner, maybe 50 metres from the hotel at a crossroads. So, I am edging out at this crossroads and as I am edging out there is a flash across me. A taxi smacks me on the side of the head and I take the full brunt. Lucy was thrown off the bike apparently and I was unconscious on the ground. That was me in a coma for six days. They thought I had died at one stage and just put me in the ambulance."

Jansen returned for Blackburn in October 2002 and netted twice in the FA Cup win over Aston Villa the following January, but after six more outings without scoring, he joined Coventry on loan in 2003. He was convinced that he has been brain damaged in the incident and this led to depression and anxiety. "I was invincible before the accident and the opposite afterwards. I was crying each night and it got worse and worse and worse. The lowest of the lows was drinking really heavily. To say I was suicidal is probably true. I was just in a horrible place and desperate to get out of it." He worked with the esteemed psychologist Steve Peters who helped him to understand what his mind was going through and what was causing his anxiety, but this didn't prevent this creeping onto the pitch with him. "Steve [Peters] believes I came back too soon. It was about four or five months. There is no criticism on Blackburn because nobody had experienced this kind of thing before. They wanted to get me back out as quickly as possible." Jansen would see out his contract with Blackburn but only make a handful of appearances in the following four years before his release in 2006, scoring only four goals. He then joined Bolton, where he only made six appearances. This would mark the end of his career at the top level, one in which so much was expected and touted after his 2001/2 season but didn't deliver. If he had gone to that World Cup who knows what could've happened. For Jansen though he is just happy that his life has managed to come full circle and escape the pits of despair he found himself in. "Anybody has bad days and good days, but I can manage my bad days and I wouldn't say they are really bad. I had horrific times but managed to come through that. Lucy [now Jansen's wife] had it worse in Rome because she saw everything. Then, my bad times of drinking and baby tantrums, she took the brunt of it really. She stood by me and managed to get me through it eventually."

Another rising English striker who had his career curtailed by injury was Malcom Christie. In 2001 he scored the winner as Derby defeated Manchester United at Old Trafford, as well as then scoring 2 goals against them in the return fixture at Pride Park, which also had a hat-trick goal incorrectly ruled out. Derby would be relegated at the end of the 2001/2 season, and it was at this time that Christie was set to join Middlesbrough for a club record fee of £6million. This however was rejected by Derby who had signed Christie from non-league Nuneaton Borough in 1997 for a small fraction of that fee, as they held out for £9million. He would therefor stay with Derby going into the championship season, before finally joining the following January for a combined fee of £3million with teammate Chris Riggot. That summer had saw Boro sign top goalscorer at the U21 European Championships Massimo Macarone, a tournament in which Christie played no minutes disappointingly for England, behind Jermaine Defoe and Peter Crouch in the pecking order. The incident which caused the start of Christie's decline would involve both his friend Riggot and Macarone.

In a training session, involving attacker's vs defenders Christie would break his leg from a tackle from his friend Riggot, who was too slow to Christie nicking the ball round him and lunged causing a leg break. Riggot was understandably devastated, as were many of his teammates. However, Riggot would later reveal that the only reason he had went in so hard is that management staff had quietly asked all defenders to go in hard on all attackers, as they were concerned how easily record signing Macarone went down in matches. Therefore, they were trying to toughen him up, but in doing so had meant that Christie would now spend an extended period on the sidelines. The injury came only five months after joining Boro. "They messed about with my injury,' he recalls. 'I don't think I was treated right, or the right decisions were made. I ended up playing and training with a broken leg, which was horrific. Then the second injury comes along. Then the third and fourth. Then it's the seventh and eighth operation. Gradually, over time, the drive and impetus drain away, and the resentment builds up. Middlesbrough being successful fed into that. They signed Mark Viduka, Jimmy Floyd Hasselbaink and Yakubu and they scored loads of goals. The fans weren't missing me because they'd won a trophy and reached the UEFA Cup final.' The trophy that they won was the Carling Cup, a cup in which Christie's goal in Extra-time in the second round ensured they made it safely through. He would be injured for the final though and would not even be allowed to celebrate with the team or receive a winner's medal for the part he played.

He would be released from Boro at the end of his contract in 2007, before then having a hugely disappointing trial at Hull, then followed by a more promising one at Leeds. there was a contract on the table, but on the day, he was to sign it, Christie broke his back, twisting to hit a shot during a routine crossing-and-finishing training session. This like we discussed before shows how unlucky some players can be. Luckily for Christie though, Leeds helped him regain fitness and, 10 months later, the same £1,000-a-game deal was still on offer. Christie signed, made his debut and scored, but things soured when Simon Grayson replaced Gary McAllister as manager. Grayson didn't want Christie around and this marked the end of his football career. "That was the moment I knew I was done with football,' he says. 'He was right, it was his decision

117

but the way it happened, in my mind, I couldn't take any more. There was no coming back. My first injury was in November 2003, that's a bloody long time to go through the torture of rejection after rejection, hurt after hurt, setback after setback. I often wonder what if the first injury finished me off. I might have got on with the rest of my life better than I did.'

During his 11-year career Christie spent half of it injured. Due to the pay as you play contract, he had signed also at Leeds he had only earned £5000 since leaving his £15,000 a week contract with Boro in 2007. "The phone stopped ringing. People there on the up were gone overnight. Nobody wanted me. I didn't even tell anyone I'd retired. I didn't need to because no one was bothered, it wasn't news. I came to resent football for years. I couldn't watch it because of the memories of what I could've done and what I could've achieved. I wasn't able to face it."

During the bad periods of his injuries, he had also lost touch with his parents, who were such a huge part of his early career and had also seen his marriage to his first wife end. "I went to the doctors and broke down in the surgery, couldn't really speak,' he says. 'I felt a little bit alone. They advised some therapy in the NHS and I had 10 sessions. I was able to open up and talk about what I talk about in the book, what I've gone through, what I felt, to someone with no preconceptions of who I was or what I'd done. That helped massively, getting some of the baggage out and away." Christie has recently released his own autobiography to outline the struggles he went through but believes what happened to him can be used as a lesson. "To know what it takes to follow your passion and achieve your dream but to know the other side, the adversity and rejection."

In a chapter that has focused on the effects that football can have on player's long-term health through injury, a whole chapter could be dedicated to the effects of heading balls on the brain function of players in later life. I have tried to focus more on injuries and the effect on players mental health during their career. But I think it must be mentioned that professional footballers aren't just at significant risk of long-term neurological effects linked to concussions and other knocks. But more worryingly are the risks of heading balls in future life causing chronic traumatic encephalopathy (a form of dementia), which was confirmed as the cause of death in former England footballer Jeff Astle in 2014. This has seen guidelines brought in at professional clubs and at grassroots level for children, reducing the number of headers they can do each week. A recent study by the University of Glasgow and Neuropathologist William Stewart and his team, saw them study the death certificates of Scottish men. What they found was very worrying for those who play football, with higher rates of dementia among former professional footballers compared to the general public. Ex-footballers are 3.5t times more likely to die from a neurodegenerative disease such as what causes dementia, rather than someone who didn't play football professionally. It was also found that dementia deaths in professional footballers, had a correlation with positions that required more frequent heading for their position, such as central defenders.

All this shows to highlight how footballers' bodies, brains and mental health is all at risk of long-term problems, all due to football. Players seek to achieve their dreams of playing at the highest level due to their love for football, but injuries are part and parcel of football and like some of those in this chapter, shows how this can lead some to the brink of ending their own life as darkness surrounds them. This is only a fraction as well of players who have suffered long-term injuries in English football, which obviously then doesn't take into consideration players from around the world. It also isn't just limited to professional footballers, as many people who play football recreationally or in amateur leagues for most of their lives will have to undergo operations themselves to correct injuries caused by football. Some in later life due to their quality of life being affected by their injuries requiring knee replacements or hip replacements for example. If told at the start of their career there is a likelihood you may never be able to walk normally after you end your career or do simple tasks, would these players still seek to achieve their dream of becoming a footballer? No amount of money earned could make player's think it is okay to be at a higher risk of suffering from dementia as they get older, which would later cause their death. Footballers are commodities to most clubs and although they will be supported in their recovery from injury, will be disposed of when it's proven they can now longer benefit the team. Football is a cutthroat business, and a player is one mistimed tackle or sometimes even a misstep before their career they have worked so hard for is taken away from them in the blink of an eye. The sport they love so much will forget them, when it is proven, they can no longer play to the same level they have always done, and then after battling to reach the top, they must have the hardest battle of their lives, their own mind and body.

5
Match-fixing

"Yes, I made mistakes in the past on the touchline. Yes, I will make less, but I think I will still make a few. But what never happened to me and will never happen is to be suspended for match-fixing"

Jose Mourinho, whilst Manchester United manager in 2018

The 'Special One', has never been a man to mince his words. If he finds an opportunity to dig at a rival or tarnish them in anyway then he will not hold back. To be successful in most things in life, there must be challenges and enemies to overcome along the way. This has been no different for the whole of Mourinho's managerial career. One of his biggest rivalries was with Pep Guardiola, to whom he was quoted as saying, "When you enjoy what you do, you don't lose your hair, and Guardiola is bald. He doesn't enjoy football." They had many head-to-heads at various clubs, with the most iconic perhaps, when his Inter side beat Barcelona at the Nou Camp. Mourinho silenced not only the Nou Camp but also Guardiola, they won the Champions League Semi-final tie before going on to win the 2010 Champions League Final. The rivalry would continue however though with many barbed comments during press conferences and arguments on the touchlines. His time in England would also see him regularly joust with Rafael Benitez and Arsene Wenger, of the latter he said, "If he is right and I am afraid of failure it is because I didn't fail many times. Eight years without silverware, that's failure." Most of these rivalries he would form would be due to the competitive nature he has to stay on top and be the best. Winning at all costs is what

Mourinho instils into his players in any way they can and that includes his battles on the touchlines to. However, the quote at the top of the page was not aimed at any of the managers we have discussed so far, but the current Tottenham manager Antonio Conte. At the time Conte was manager of Mourinho's former team Chelsea, a team he led to their first ever Premier League title and had previously been a hero to all Chelsea fans. But Mourinho left his past loyalties behind when he returned as Manchester United manager, and adoration soon changed to hate. He made Chelsea fans feel how Liverpool and Arsenal fans had felt towards him as he attacked their manager in the press, and they supported Conte as their rivalry ignited. The fuel that started the fire inside Mourinho was his perception that Conte over celebrated during a 4-0 thrashing by Chelsea of Manchester United at Stamford Bridge. It led to Mourinho dubbing him the 'Clown of the touchline'. But back to the original quote at the beginning of the chapter, was this mind games or was their truth behind his attack.

In reference to the remarks by Mourinho, Conte responded angrily by calling him a "little man". Although, Mourinho's comments weren't wholly true, as Conte was never accused of match-fixing, it was however claimed that he was aware of two attempts to do so and didn't alert the relevant authorities. The charges come from the former Italian manager's time as Siena manager between May 2010 and May 2011. This was just before he took over as Juventus manager. The scandal was referred to in Italy as Calcio Scommesse. It was a betting scandal that came to light in 2011, during Operation:Last Bet. The allegations were all based on the testimony of former Siena player Filippo Carobbio. He claimed that a match against Novara in April 2011 was fixed to end in a draw. The reason for this was that Siena President Massimo Mezzaroma had placed a significant sum of money on a draw. The game finished 2-2.

Carobbio said that the owner was not only complicit in this though, but that Conte was fully aware of the plot. "There was an agreement for the draw, and, in fact, we speak about it during our technical meeting," he stated in 2012. "We were all aware of the agreed outcome, above all so that we could act accordingly during the game. The coach himself, Antonio Conte, told us that we could rest easy as we had reached an agreement with Novara." Carobbio didn't end there though with his allegations against Conte. He also said that Conte was aware of a second occasion of match-fixing against AlbinoLeffe, where once again an attempt to arrange a result was made, towards the end of the same season. This time Carobbio said that him and a teammate Claudio Terri, were told by assistant coach Cristian Stelleni in January 2011, to approach players from AlbinoLeffe to, "make arrangements for the return game, so that the points would go to the side with the greater need." It would turn out that Siena were promoted from Serie B come the return fixture, whilst their opponents were battling relegation. The game saw AlbinoLeffe win 1-0, a result which left some players not happy, as it would mean they couldn't finish first in the league and receive the maximum bonus they could. "However, in the end, we all agreed, the team and the coach, to give the win to AlbinoLeffe."

Conte was cleared of any wrongdoing in relation to the Novara fixture, but it was found that he was aware of the attempt against AlbinoLeffe and didn't report this to the authorities. Conte denied he had any knowledge of illegal activities taking place, but his lawyer advised him to take a plea bargain that would see him banned from the touchstone for 3 months, but without having to admit any guilt. However, this proposal was rejected by the Italian Football Federation. This was to the surprise of Conte who said, "I agree with the judges on one thing: 90 days wasn't a suitable punishment - the right one is zero," he argued. "Even if today, I had the certainty of a three-month ban, my answer would have been 'no'. I didn't do anything illegal, and I didn't fail to report anything." Due to the rejection of his first plea bargain he rejected the opportunity to negotiate a second time with the Football federation and said he didn't even want to do it the first time but had been forced by the prosecutors to. "I consider a plea-bargain blackmail," he fumed. "I'm an innocent person yet I'm told by my lawyer to plea bargain. It's embarrassing. They have ruined my credibility in the changing room. Those people who know me know what type of person Antonio Conte is.".

The case hinged on one man's word against another's. Even though some questioned the credibility of Carobbio and the fact that no other players backed up his version of events. This was enough for Conte to be banned for ten months and see his ban be upheld by the Italian Federal Court. The ban would mean that he would now be banned from the touch line for the majority of his first season as manager of Juventus. This infuriated both Conte and Juventus. They appealed his ban once more and this time National Court for Sports Arbitration, reduced his ban to four months. This meant that he missed most of the first half of the 2012-13 season and watched on from the stands. Conte continued to protest his innocence, but prosecutors didn't buy the fact that he wasn't aware of his assistants plans to fix the AlbinoLeffe match. His role had cost him a two-and-a-half-year ban. Prosecutors then pressed ahead with criminal charges, and this saw Conte charged with Sporting Fraud in 2016. The timing was terrible as Conte was set to lead Italy to the European Championships in France that summer, therefore fast tracked the case to take place before the tournament. Prosecutors wanted him to receive a suspended 6-month sentence and hefty fine.

However, he was ultimately found not guilty, with Judge Pierpaolo Beluzzi ruling the case against the Azzurri coach "baseless".

Conte issued this statement on his Facebook page after being found to be innocent, showing how the ordeal had affected him. "Four years ago, with the search which took place in my home at five o'clock in the morning, began a nightmare which at times I thought I could never finish," he wrote.
"[Those who I am] close to and know me, know how much I've suffered at the very idea that we could pull over my name to the shame of Calcio Scommesse. Today finally puts an end to this ugly story. As I have always said, even to those who were called upon to judge me, I'm a man of sport and I don't know any other way to get to success if not through sacrifice and total dedication. It's been a terrible experience that I faced with my head held high. It shows the path that I've decided to undertake within the process, without looking for comfortable loopholes as I have always done in life and in sport. To all those who have never doubted my loyalty, I want to express my gratitude, and to reassure that from this test came out a stronger person and even more motivated."

So, although Mourinho's jibes were somewhat true as Conte had been suspended for events surrounding match-fixing. He was eventually proved to be innocent and from his statement showed how emotional a time this was for him. Maybe therefore Mourinho chose this topic as an insult, as he knew it would hurt Conte personally. It would also make those in England unaware of the events to question his morals. Match fixing and cheating is seen by many as one of the lowest things you could do in sport. It takes away from the unrivalled excitement of uncertainty that football creates and makes so many of us love the sport. In the above case the match fixing didn't affect a team's results positively but was more fuelled by the greed of an owner and supporting a

125

team's survival. However, match fixing has often be used to ensure a team wins. This section of the book is titled 'To win at all costs" and match fixing is the method that has been used by some to ensure this.

If you were to ask someone born after the millennium, who are the only French team to win the Champions League; the answer would probably be Paris Saint-Germain (PSG). Which of course for anyone born before the millennium, is incorrect. Although they won the UEFA cup winners cup in 1996, the nearest they have got to winning Europe's premier competition was in 2020, when they were beat by Bayern Munich. It's probably lost on the younger generation that PSG were only formed in 1970. They won their first league title in 1986 and had a hugely successful period in the 1990's, before a decline during the 2000's. They're known now as the dominant side in French football. Their fortunes changed in 2011, when they were taken over by the Emir of Qatar, through closed shareholder Qatar Sports Investments. They instantly became the richest club in French football and one of the richest in the world. The unparalleled finances at their disposal have made them dominate domestic competitions, with the likes of Messi, Neymar and Mbappe, making the league look like a training session. But even with these players at their disposal, the UEFA champions league has still avoided them. Instead, the French team that has been successful in winning the Champions League, is their fiercest rivals Olympique de Marseille; the duo contest French football's most notorious match, Le Classique. Although fortunes have favoured PSG recently, making them the most popular team in France, Marseille's fortunes have not matched that of their great rivals.

Former Marseille player and member of the 1993 Champions League winning side said this about Marseille, "There isn't a city like it in England really, nowhere with a similar type of civic behaviour. It's quite like Napoli in that has a sort-of Latin mentality. There's lots of immigrants, lots of people who don't have a lot of money. But it's such a special place, and football has the capability in these places to really change things—to make a city feel magnificent. Even if you are sat in your room with a TV and a beer and the kids are running around, these football moments can give you the ability to forget any problems."

The club's motto, "Droit au but", dates from the days when the club's main sport was rugby, under the name "Football Club de Marseille", translated it means "Straight to the Goal". The badge then features an O and a M, the abbreviation of Olympique de Marseille. Above that, is then a sole star, representing their Champions League victory. The best spell in the history of the club was from the late 1980s to the mid 1990s. Bernard Tapie became the president of the club and constructed the greatest team ever witnessed in France, to that date. The Qatari-rich PSG would arguably lay claim to that now. Tapie signed players such as Alain Giresse, Jean-Pierre Papin, Chris Waddle, Klaus Allofs, Enzo Francescoli, Abedi Pelé, Didier Deschamps, Basile Boli, Marcel Desailly, Rudi Völler and Eric Cantona. He also appointed high-profile coaches like Franz Beckenbauer, Gérard Gili and Raymond Goethals. Between 1989 and 1992 Marseille won four consecutive French league titles and this period then climaxed with them winning, the UEFA Champions League in its new format in 1993.

But although this was the most successful period in the club's history on the pitch, it is remembered by others less fondly. Arsenal Wenger, when discussing this period of French football in 2006 to L'Equipe said this. "We are talking about the worst period French football has been through. It was gangrenous, from the inside, because of the influence and methods of Tapie and Marseille". Wenger who was Monaco manager during the Tapie era said this was "The most difficult period of his life". In 2013 he went on to say, "There were little incidents, that added one to the other, in the end there is no coincidence. But it's very difficult to prove." This anger almost boiled over once during this period as Wenger was restrained from confronting Tapie in the tunnel after a defeat to his Marseille team. So was this hatred based on jealousy on Wenger's behalf towards Tapie and his Marseille team or was there sinister reasons for his ill feeling towards him.

"Tapie is a person who knows no limits. He would do anything to get to the top." These are the words of Marc Fratani to Le Monde, the man who was Tapie's henchmen in the early 90's. Tapie was a driven, out-spoken character, eager to see his side succeed at any cost...literally. Fratani continued his confessional to Le Monde. "I once attended a meeting to buy a referee, it was for a game against PSG in Paris," continued Fratani, whose nickname was L'homme de l'ombre, 'Man of the Shadows'. "In that game, we also conditioned our opponent with Haldol [a drug usually used in the treatment of schizophrenia, Tourette syndrome, and mania in bipolar disorder]. We added it using syringes with an ultra-thin needle. We injected it into plastic bottles, and anything they ate or drank from was treated with it." However, those incidences aren't what Tapie will be remembered for most, that would transpire a week before the biggest game in Marseille's history. The Champions League was the one thing Tapie desired most, and his desperation would lead him to take drastic measures to ensure they could retain their Ligue 1 title at the same time. As the final approached, the league title was still undecided with Marseille top, but with challengers closely following them.

The previous season's disappointing exit from the Champions League at the hands of Sparta Prague, saw Tapie splash the cash to ensure the same outcome would not follow in the 1993 tournament. He signed a raft of big names, including Fabien Barthez, Marcel Desailly, Alen Boksic and World Cup-winning striker Rudi Voller. These new signings alongside the players who had allowed them to win the previous four French league titles, had propelled them to the brink of being double winners of the league and European's premier competition. The incident which would ultimately see Tapie's notoriety reach an all-time high came the weekend before the Champions League final against AC Milan in Munich. Marseille travelled to Valenciennes in a must-win game to see them lift the league before their all-important final. Marseille won the league game 1-0, but what surprised many was the lacklustre performance from their opponents. Suspicions were first raised at half-time in the game when Valenciennes player Jacques Glassmann told coach Boro Primorac that he had been offered money to "lift his foot" by both Marseille player Jean-Jacques Eydelie, a former team-mate at Nantes, and Marseille director Jean-Pierre Bernes.

However, it turned out that he was not the only player who had been approached, with the offer of money to aid Marseille in their quest for League glory. A bag of money would later be discovered in the back garden of player Christophe Robert's mother-in-law (Look's far too close to my name for my liking, I don't want any part of what he did or be wrongly accused of being part of this story). This money would start an investigation that would tarnish not only the reputation of Tapie but also that of Marseille forever. It was later found that Christophe and teammate Jorge Burruchaga (an Argentine who scored the winning goal in the 1986 World Cup Final) had also been offered money to allow Marseille an easy passage of victory, but their approach had come before the game started. The money that was found in Robert's mother-in-law's garden was collected by his wife, who collected a bag full of money from the car park of Marseille's team hotel. Criminal investigations would be opened on June 8th and would lead to months of claims and counterclaims. All this just a few weeks after not only Marseilles greatest victory but also French football's greatest ever victory.

The man in the dugout for much of this period was Raymond Goethals and on that night in Munich he would organise and motivate his team to defeat, perhaps the greatest defence the game has ever known. This AC Milan team has already been discussed earlier in the book. But it is important to remember the magnitude of the task they faced. They were up against one of the all-time great sides who had only just started to decline from their commanding peak. Fabio Capello's team still contained Dutch maestros Frank Rijkaard and Marco van Basten and a defensive line that included Alessandro Costacurta, Franco Baresi, and Paolo Maldini. Goethals setup his team to frustrate Milan, much like they had done to many over the previous years. Their plan was to soak up the pressure of Milan and then threaten from set-pieces and using the pace of Voller to threaten on the counterattack. It would be a set-piece that would bring the only goal of the game. The goal came in the 42nd minute of the match, after a marauding run, from OM's Ghanaian winger Abedi Pele. Abedi Pele is believed by some to be the greatest African player of all-time and is the father of Ghanaian premier league starts Andre and Jordan Ayew. He would take the corner that would be met at the front post by Basile Boli, with his header flying past Milan keeper Sebastiano Rossi into the corner of the net. Centre-back Boli would describe his goal as, "It was a header for eternity."

The goal may not be remembered for eternity by many but the repercussions of what happened from the aftermath of the Valenciennes incident would be remembered by the whole of French football for eternity. Due to the criminal investigations, Marseille was unable to defend their Champions League title the following year by UEFA. Interestingly though they were never stripped of their title. It took then until the following April for the French FA to condemn Marseille to relegation, whilst they say in second place behind eventual champions PSG. Months after their relegation they had to file for bankruptcy, and it would take until 1996 and the takeover by Adidas owner Robert Louis-Dreyfus to improve their finances enough to allow them to be promoted back to Ligue 1. Tapie was sentenced to two years in jail, including eight months non-suspended, for complicity of corruption and subornation of witnesses. Bernes, who has since become an agent, was handed a similar punishment, albeit with just three weeks non-suspended. Eydelie the player involved in the on-field corruption was given a one-year suspended prison sentence and served 17 days behind bars but was banned from footballing activities for 18 months. This would see his career ended just as it reached its peak and never regain the heights he reached during his time at Marseille. He would eventually find himself at Walsall before retiring in 2001.

However, the controversy around the whole situation would start again in 2006, when Eydelie released an autobiography that then brought into question the previously untarnished Champions League victory. In his 2006 autobiography he claimed that prior to the meeting with Milan, he and several other players were given suspicious injections. Due to the time that had transpired between the match and these allegations there was little UEFA could do to investigate these accusations except check that anti-doping tests had taken place. "Those tests proved negative," FFF president

131

Jean-Pierre Escalettes and LFP president Frederic Thiriez said in a joint statement as the controversy resurfaced with a bang. Tapie even tried to sue the player due to the comments he had made but was unsuccessful. If found to have been true then the Champions League title they had been allowed to keep, may have been retrospectively taken off them, meaning no French side had ever one the Champions League. Mundial magazine describe this period perfectly as this, "as French football's Lance Armstrong moment, and their trophies and achievements may be scratched out—as some have already been—but for a long-suffering city continuously patronised by Paris, what can't be removed are the memories of what this time represented." This and the will to be the best and win at all costs is what led Tapie to use these underhand and morally wrong tactics, but I feel that Champions League victory and still being the only French team to lift the cup will be vindication for him and his actions. The unparalleled success they had in that period would never be matched by themselves again and it is now their rivals who have a stranglehold over French football like they once did. They have one solitary league title in 2010 led by Didier Deschamps and a losing effort in the Europa League final in 2018 under Rudi Garcia. They may never reach them heights again, but Tapie delivered what the Qatari billions have yet to do for PSG, however big a shadow is cast on their achievements.

Bribery, kidnap, and fraud were all charges floated against what Italian prosecutors described as a sophisticated criminal organisation. Yet these were not the charges levied against the fearsome Italian Mafia, but against various Italian football clubs, with the head of the supposed organisation being the 'old lady' Juventus. This nickname is translated from the Italian '*Vecchia Signora*', they have been run by the industrial Angelli family almost continuously since 1923, making them the oldest and longest dynasty in national sports. In 2009, the club were ranked the second best in the 20th century based on a statistical study series by the International Federation of Football History and Statistics, making them the highest-ranking Italian team. The club has provided the most players to the Italian National team in official competitions, mostly uninterrupted since 1924. With these squads seeing the Azzuri, achieve world champions status on 3 occasions. The most recent of these being in 2006. Juventus are the second oldest active team in Italian football behind only Genoa. They have competed in the top division of Italian football for all but one season in 2006-07. This year and the World Cup success in 2006, would see the culmination of a criminal investigation that would change the landscape of Italian football forever.

Roberto Beccantini, a correspondent for La Stampa newspaper in Italy, said that in 2006 and the build-up to the World Cup in Germany that, "Many of the politicians, journalists and showmen decided to cheer against our national team." The backdrop to the tournament, saw the Italian National team captain and Juventus player Fabio Cannavaro, summoned to Rome to bear witness to allegations of 'illegal competition with use of threats and violence'. He was accompanied by Juventus teammate and France striker David Trezeguet. More seriously though, their club teammate and Italy's outstanding number one Gianluigi Buffon was being threatened with more serious charges of, 'involvement in illegal betting on domestic games'. These allegations and investigations looming over the players didn't affect the Italians though, who managed to focus their attentions on becoming world champions. Cannavaro would lift the cup for the Azzuri, with Buffon performing heroics in a penalty shootout against France. Their teammate Trezeguet would not be as successful though, as he missed the crucial penalty in the shootout, that allowed Italy to secure the crown. The game itself is probably remembered mostly for the exit of one of the greatest players to grace a football pitches, acrimonious exits from football. France captain Zinidine Zidane, a former Juventus player himself, had given his team an early lead from the penalty spot. However, he gave Italy all the momentum to go on and lift the cup, after falling for the dark arts of Italy Centre-Back Marco Materazzi, who is reported to have insulted Zidane's mother and sister. The reaction was exactly what Materazzi, would have wished for in his wildest dreams. He probably didn't plan for the pain he felt, but the reaction shocked the whole world. The head butt to the centre of Materazzi's chest, who was never shy to go down easy, but rightly this time sent him tumbling to the floor in a heap. Zidane exited the world's biggest stage, in the world's biggest game in disgrace.

Without his mercurial talents France's chances of lifting the World Cup ended and with it the fairy tale exit for one of the world's best ever players. The whole incident was beamed all over the world news, yet this news would diminish due to the storm that was brewing in Italian football. Members of the Italian team were flying back home to face investigators, basically accusing them of being corrupt. For the first time in history, the nation that had just been crowned world champions and some of the star names that had made this possible; were flying back to investigators, who were accusing them of being corrupt.

How these accusations and investigations came about were from rumours that had been circulating from 2004. The rumours came from both publics hear-say but also Camorra leaks to government officials in Naples. The original rumours, however, were never found to be true. The first was that Juventus players were susceptible to doping and this was going unpunished or was too sophisticated to be caught by doping agencies at that time. The second was that illegal betting was taking place in the sport and this also included corrupt referees involved in this. A task force was therefore setup to investigate these claims, using wiretaps on some of the biggest and most powerful names in Italian football. What came out in these wiretaps however would be something much bigger than the investigators could ever have predicted: Calciopoli.

Calciopoli, loosely translates to English as 'Footballgate'. The scandal would encapsulate five Serie A teams including some of the biggest teams in Italian football, they were: Juve, AC Milan, Fiorentina, Lazio and Reginna. This would all come to ahead in Spring 2006, when Turin magistrates decided to leak the information found in these wiretaps to the press. They did this after their suspicions about the Italian football governing bodies involvement in the whole scandal came to light after initially approaching them, before realising they was implicated themselves. Another reason they had to turn to the press, was the fact that AC Milan's owner at the time was the Italian President at the time Silvio Berlusconi, who due to his club's involvement, didn't want a public investigation. It therefore became front page news across Italy. The evidence although substantial from the wiretaps was still inconclusive. At the centre of it all was the Juventus Sporting Director Luciano Moggi. The wiretaps showed him communicating to the referee designators of Serie A, reportedly to reflect results in Juve's favour by selecting favourable referees for not only their own matches but also those of rivals matches. It was said that through his influence of selection of referees for rivals' games, that throughout the season, top players of rival clubs were shown a calculated number of yellow cards in a bid to ensure their suspension when their teams faced the record Italian champions. It was through recorded conversations Moggi had with the head of national referees' association, Pierluigi 'Gigi' Pairetto, clearly showing they preferred

some referees for Juventus games, that this system came to light. There was said to be 3 stages of this for Moggi:
1- choose referees he knew would favour Juventus.
2- punish those referees he felt had treated his team unfairly or given unfavourable decisions against them.
3- use referees in other games to yellow card players to ensure they were suspended when they came to play Juventus.

On top of this he also used the media to pressurise officials also. This came to light in another recorded wiretap. Conversations between Moggi and Italy's most famous sports commentator Fabio Baldas (on 18 October 2005) showed how Baldas pre-decided to make a referee (Rodomonti) look bad with his comments during the match between AC Milan and Cagliari. He used the media to conceal any bias that may be shown to Juventus, whilst also trying to pressurise officials who he felt favoured his rivals. He knew that many people's opinions were formed by sports broadcasters, especially ones such as household names like Baldas. According to investigators, Baldas and Moggi spoke before every programme to discuss what was going to be said and shown, and which referees and officials would be shone in a good or bad light. The accusations by investigators didn't stop there though or become any less farfetched. They had allegedly detained referee Gianluca Paparesta and his two assistants in a changing room after Juve's 2-1 loss at Reggina in November 2004 and were said to have berated the officials for not favouring Juve during the game. They deny this was the case. Italian newspapers also printed wiretaps of Moggi allegedly attempting to put pressure on the vice-chairman of Uefa's referees' commission and of calls made to government minister Giuseppe Pisanu. More evidence of the stranglehold he had on Italian football came just before the start of the successful 2006 World Cup as well. Italian coach Marcelo Lippi appeared in front of magistrates to answer charges that his selection of players for Italian World Cup squad had been influenced by Moggi. It was alleged that Moggi had put pressure on Lippi to select fewer Juventus players so that it would minimise the risk of injury to his players but also ensure they were fresh for the new season. The investigation was originally being called 'Moggipoli' due to the influence Moggi had on Italian football. However, through the investigations Moggi wasn't the only one calling in favours. Officials at Milan, Lazio & Fiorentina were all guilty of influencing the choice of referees too. Why had the referees been influenced by these clubs? The reason being they had no choice and were caught up in a corrupt system. If they didn't favour Juventus and they upset Moggi, it could see them losing their jobs or being demoted to lesser fixtures or lower leagues. The same applied to keeping the other clubs in the investigation happy too. The punishments the clubs received can be seen in the table below: (courtesy of BBC sport)

The sanctions

	Original punishment	Final punishment	Other punishments
Juventus	Relegated to Serie B, -30 points	Relegated to Serie B, -9 points	Stripped of 2004-05 Serie A title, downgraded to bottom of 2005-06 table
AC Milan	-15 points	-8 points	Deducted 30 points from 2005-06 season
Fiorentina	Relegated to Serie B, -12 points	-15 points in Serie A	Out of 2006-07 Champions League
Lazio	Relegated to Serie B, -7 points	-3 points in Serie A	Out of 2006-07 Uefa Cup
Reggina	-15 points	-11 points	€100,000 fine

Although the news had been leaked to the media which then caused the storm that saw the full investigation take place and the punishments be handed down. The leaks also worked against investigators as it took away the momentum in their case and didn't allow them to continue to collect evidence against Moggi and others. Prosecutors were very confident of criminal convictions against some including Moggi at the start of police interviews, as it was clear Moggi and others were completely unaware of the investigation. But as the leaks continued their confidence grew and once again Moggi used his contacts in other sections of the media to paint himself as a scapegoat and that he wasn't the only one doing it, which was supported vigorously by those in Turin.

Moggi was charged with attempted sporting fraud – but the attempts were found to be completely unsuccessful in altering the results. It was found that the 2004/05 season was not altered by any illicit means and meant Juventus were able to hold on to their league title from this season. The proceedings in the High Court also found, that Moggi was far from alone in his attempts at unlawful behaviour. New evidence indicated similar dubious actions from the directors of Milan and Inter among others. It took a further nine years after the case came into the spotlight, the Italian Supreme Court (Corte di Cassazione) gave the final verdict on the case. Moggi was acquitted of "some individual charges for sporting fraud, but not from being the 'promoter' of the 'criminal conspiracy' that culminated in Calciopoli." The remaining charges on him were cancelled without a new trial due to the statute of limitations. He never served a day in prison although he was banned from having any role in Italian football for life. Appeals by Fiorentina owners Andrea and Diego Della Valle and Lazio President Claudio Lotito against their sentences were also rejected on the ground that their cases passed the statute of limitations. Three of the referees indicted in the case had their charges dropped on appeal, although two referees Massimo De Santis and Salvatore Racabulto had theirs upheld. A 150- page document was released by the Supreme Court in 2015, in it, it was made clear that, Moggi's unwarranted activities incurred significant damage to Italian football not only in a sporting sense but also in economic terms.

Moggi remained hidden in the shadows until the release of Netflix's Documentary series "Bad Sport' looked at Calciopolli in an episode titled 'Footballgate'. In it Moggi finally broke his silence on how he felt he was treated in the aftermath of the revelations being released to the press, whilst also still pleading his innocence. He said this in the documentary, 'I thought about suicide in the first days after the Calciopoli news. Only faith in God saved me, I had become everyone's target. The system did not exist, but only I had to pay. I was no longer serene, and I was also ashamed to walk the streets and at that moment I thought about many things, including suicide,' he adds. 'Yes, in the first days after the news and the great media hype I thought about suicide to put an end to everything. Then, thanks to faith in God, I found immense strength and continued to this day with a lot of commitment.' Although he denies his involvement, the wiretaps contradict this. All this came down to winning at all costs. Moggi had a quest to make Juventus Italy's most successful team, and this meant winning by any means necessary. However, his ban from the sport he loved so much for life and the media character assassination made him consider taking his own life. So even though he achieved his aim of winning league titles (although stripped of two of these titles and given to Inter), we must question was this all worth it for Moggi. By trying to take away the uncertainty of winning at all costs, he led himself to a decline in his mental health and contemplating taking his own life.

Away from Moggi though, Juventus would return to Serie A at the first time of trying. Some of the world's biggest international stars and best of their era stuck by the teams even in the lower division. Buffon, Del Piero, Giorgio Chiellini, Pavel Nedved and David Trezeguet all decided to stay with Juve. This didn't mean they didn't lose some of their biggest stars to some of Europe's giants. Zlatan Ibrahimovic and Patrick Vieira joined rivals Inter Milan for a combined £23m, Fabio Cannavaro and Emerson went to Real Madrid for a total of £13.7m, Lilian Thuram and Gianluca Zambrotta joined Barcelona for £13m, while Adrian Mutu went to Fiorentina for £5.5m. without these players and also a minus nine point start they still became champions, losing only four games all season. Juventus have now reclaimed some form of dominance on Italian football reaching a Champions League final in 2014-15 and winning numerous league titles, although Inter and Milan have won the previous two competitions.

An interesting side story of the whole Calciopolli scandal is the team that benefitted most from the whole situation…. Inter. They would be given the titles taken off Juventus, which to Juve fans is known as 'Scudetto di Cartone', the cardboard title. Rumours are also rife of Inter president Massimo Moratti's involvement in the media storm it created. He had control of the newspapers: Corriere dello sport, Contro Campo, Messagero and la Gazzetta dello Sport, all some of the main papers to leak the tapes to the public. Other accusations also come against the investigation, were the new commissioner of `Italian football who had not been implicated in any tapes was announced as Guido Rossi. The issue with this was that he didn't declare he happened to be a major investor in Inter and a former delegate for the club who used to sit next to Moratti during games. He not only controlled the proceedings but also picked the jury. The Italian football federation realised this conflict of interest too late, and all punishments had already been handed down. When they did come to light though he was asked to step down as commissioner. The new Juve delegates attempted further appeals to overturn their verdicts but were blackmailed into dropping it. FIFA announced that it had the option to suspend the Italian football federation, which would freeze all Italian competition (even international duty) if the appeal took place. Juve had no choice but to drop it. Due to lost revenues on Milan and Juventus' sides, Inter were in a monopoly position on the market that allowed them to purchase players the other clubs couldn't afford as well as the players Juve were forced to sell. This period of superiority would culminate in Inter winning a famous treble in 2009-10, winning the League, the Coppa Italia and UEFA Champions league. The title was also their fifth consecutive title including the carboard scudetto. Even though the same accusations were levied against Inter, they were the only top team not to face punishment.

PART II

GREED

6
Gambling

"I've been addicted to alcohol and cocaine, but the most destructive and only one I'm still struggling with is gambling"

Paul Merson in BBC documentary in 2022

Paul Merson is one of the most recognisable faces in football to have admitted his problems with gambling. Throughout his career he has struggled with addictions to alcohol and cocaine, that led him to be using cocaine on the way to training sessions in the back of taxis, straight from nights out. But gambling is something he has struggled more than the others to stop. "If I want to get drunk or high, I must put something up my nose or down me. Gambling's already in you, just waiting constantly, talking to you." It is something that he is still battling with and struggling with this to the present day. "I placed my first bet at 16 and lost my entire first month's wages at Arsenal in ten minutes at William Hill. And I didn't stop until, eventually, I'd lost everything I'd ever had – close to £7 million, including houses, cars, marriages, my entire pension and my self-respect." It has recently come out in the press that Merson has once again relapsed during lockdown. This time once again the temptation to bet took over and left him losing a deposit he had saved for a house he was buying for his wife Kate and their three children. On this occasion he lost £160,000 betting during the Covid-19 pandemic. His sport of choice, table tennis. A sport that he had no knowledge of but due to the lockdown on other sports, was the only thing he could bet on. This was due to the anxiety he faced from being furloughed from his job and worrying about when he would be able to return to work. With time on his hands, although enjoying spending time with his family, adverts on TV tempted him in once again even though as any gambler knows there was only one outcome. "I'd be sitting on the sofa, and I'd look over at the kids," he says. "The hate I had for myself, thinking about how I'd let them down. The scary thing is you know there's only one outcome, but you can't stop."

Merson is a huge advocate for gambling controls and has recently filmed a documentary about the risks of gambling and how gambling companies are not doing enough to stop people losing all they have, like what has happened to Merson and many others. A study conducted for the Professional Players' Federation in 2014 showed 6.1% of sportsmen would be classed as problem gamblers, compared with 1.9% in the general population of young men. Merson believes the nature of a footballer's lifestyle makes them more susceptible to having a problem with gambling. "I think you've got bundles of money and bundles of time," he says. This is something that was supported by former Manchester United, Newcastle and Northern Ireland international Keith Gillespie. Like Merson he estimates he has lost around £7million due to his gambling addiction. Gillespie was declared bankrupt in 2010 following a petition by HM Revenue and Customs Commissioners over a £137,000 tax bill. The ex-winger once lost £62,000 on football and horse racing in the space of two days back in October 1995, a period he calls Black Friday, and warns he won't be the only footballer to fall into the trap. "You finish training, and in the afternoon you go home and, if you're not married, you're probably going home to an empty house or a hotel room," he recalls. So, the only thing he could do to relieve the boredom was to go to the bookies. Now, with internet accounts and telephone services, he says it's even easier to put down big stakes. "There has been plenty of publicity about players with gambling problems, but I guarantee you that there are a lot more out there who have not been named yet," he added. His betting disease stemmed from the loneliness of being a young 19-year-old with no family around and boredom that leads young footballers to spend excess amounts betting. Football and footballers have always had an unhealthy obsession with betting, something highlighted by Gillespie in the fact that he was introduced to betting when he had Sir Alex Ferguson giving him money to go put bets on for him as a young first teamer for Manchester United.

This chapter was one of the most interesting chapters to write for me as it gave me a greater insight into the risks of betting, but more importantly the role that betting companies have in dragging people to the despair felt by the likes of Merson and Gillespie. Speaking from a personal point of view I feel like betting is something that is enshrined in British working-class culture, or it has certainly felt that way for me growing up. Throughout my life betting has probably seen its greatest advances from being conducted solely in shops, to the introduction of online betting and machine terminals within shops. From a young age I felt like betting has always been around me, which now that I think about it probably isn't the best thing for a young child and is the main cause of why I bet on a weekly basis to this day and have done since I was able to do this legally at 18. I'm not sure if this is just a Liverpool thing or is a ritual that is copied around the UK, but my introduction to betting came through betting on the Grand National. My dad would come home with the newspaper with all the runners and would then queue up for around 30 minutes to an hour on the Saturday of the race putting the whole families' bets on. He would ring my Nan and Grandad to get their bets and would then put bets on for My mum, brother and sisters. Even now, after you read this chapter about the horrors of betting will I do this with my kids? Then the answer will probably be yes, this was something we loved as kids and brings you altogether to sit and watch the race and hopefully win. But it also shows from a young age that you are bearing witness to people winning and losing money on something with no fixed outcome. I thought about how else I was exposed to betting and some I didn't even think about. We would go to my Nan's caravan in Rhyl and go the arcade and bet on the horse racing machines and the other numerous machines. This was also then followed by hours spent in the prize bingo, spending money to win tokens that bought absolute Sh***.

I wish the adult in me now would tell me to not waste this money given to us and save it up, but it was clear that the alure of winning had grabbed us already and that desire to win might be the trigger for worst things to come for some people. I know many reading this will probably have been through these same experiences as a child and don't consider themselves to have a problem with gambling but what writing this chapter made me question is, is this normal? I would then get a few quid to bet on a first goal scorer if I was out with my dad watching the match or put my name down on a spot the ball. A race comes on the television in the pub and an impromptu sweep is made with the winner takes all. This is what I've grew up with and whenever one of these things happened it would excite me and, in some ways, will still now. But although I loved doing all these things with my dad and to many this may be normal, to others maybe not, I highly doubt that this happens anywhere else in the world except for the UK. I am surrounded by people who bet on a regular basis and there aren't many people I know who don't have a bet on the weekend. It is part of people's weekly routines, one that has been made so easier by having it all at your fingertips, which is something I have felt has seen me change my own routines and bet on more than one day a week. Every month you are also likely to get a 'flair' message of a guaranteed tip that somebody knows is going to win as well.

The UK has one of the biggest gambling markets in the world, generating a profit of £14.2 billion in 2020. Previous research has shown that harms associated with gambling are wide-ranging. These include not only harms to the individual gambler but their families, close associates, and wider society There have been growing calls by the public health community, people with lived experience and parliamentarians that a population-level approach is needed to tackle this public health issue. In 2018, 24.5 million people in England gambled (54% of the adult population, or 40% when you exclude the National Lottery). The National Lottery is the most common type of gambling across all age groups, except among younger people where scratch cards are more common. Football pools and electronic gaming machines are more common among people under 35 years of age compared with older age groups.

Based on 2018 data, it was estimated that 0.5% of the population reached the threshold to be considered problem gamblers, and this proportion has remained relatively consistent since 2012. It was also estimated that 3.8% of the population are classified as at-risk gamblers. These people are typically low- or moderate-risk gamblers, meaning they may experience some level of negative consequences due to their gambling. The highest rates of gambling participation are among people who have higher academic qualifications, people who are employed, and among relatively less deprived groups. People who are classified as at-risk and problem gamblers are more typically male and in younger age groups. The socio-demographic profile of gamblers appears to change as gambling risk increases, with harmful gambling associated with people who are unemployed and among people living in more deprived areas. This suggests harmful gambling is related to health inequalities. The betting companies' prey on these statistics, and gambling shops are concentrated in the most deprived areas of Britain. 21% of Britain's gambling shops are in the poorest tenth of the country. When you compare this to the most affluent areas, it is only 2%. Glasgow has the most betting shops, where the ratio is one shop for every 3,264 people. The number of betting shops in the United Kingdom gradually decreased in the past four years, however. As of September 2020, there were 6,735 betting shops in the country. This shows a drop from the previous period, most likely because of the coronavirus (COVID-19) pandemic but also the growth in mobile betting will have influenced this too. What some people are also unaware of though is that land-based gambling, as opposed to online, still accounts for about 44% of the £10.2bn of gamblers' losses in Britain every year.

Around 7% of the population of Great Britain (adults and children) were found to be negatively affected by someone else's gambling according to the best available evidence from YouGov. Affected others are more likely to be women. The most severe impacts of problem gambling were felt most by immediate family members. Almost half (48%) of people who were affected by a spouse or partner's gambling reported a severe negative impact. This was followed by people affected by the gambling of a parent (41%) and the gambling of a child (38%).

The overall estimated excess cost of health harms is estimated to be £961.3 million. This is based on the direct costs to government of treating depression, alcohol dependence and illicit drug use, as well as the wider societal costs of suicide. The estimated excess cost of suicide is £619.2 million (with 95% confidence that the

148

precise estimate is between £366.6 million and £1.1 billion), based on the wider social costs of an estimated 409 suicides associated with problem gambling.

The estimated excess cost of depression is £335.5 million (with 95% confidence that the precise estimate is between £221.7 million and £529.6 million), based on an estimated 212,511 people with depression and problem or at-risk gambling. The estimated excess cost of alcohol dependence is £4.7 million (with 95% confidence that the precise estimate is between £3.6 million and £5.7 million), based on an estimated 3,646 people receiving alcohol treatment in England. An estimated 28,312 people are both alcohol dependent and problem or at-risk gamblers. The estimated excess cost of illicit drug use is £2.0 million (with 95% confidence that the precise estimate is between £1.4 million and £2.7 million), based on an estimated 712 people receiving drug treatment. It is estimated that 1,487 people aged 17 to 24 years who are at-risk and problem gamblers also have problematic drug use in England. Another concerning statistic is that half of the 348 gambling treatment services mapped by researchers were within five minutes' walk of a gambling premises.

Gambling in the UK is a much bigger problem than many may be aware of though, and if they are aware choose to ignore the risks of gambling as so many people do it. The most damning fact and one that sticks with me more than any is the fact that one person a day dies in the UK from a gambling-related suicide. Gambling is taking people to the depths of despair and causes them to feel there is no way out, so they feel their only option is to kill themselves. Gambling is an addiction and therefore an illness, so therefore anybody can become addicted to gambling if exposed to it enough. But what is more concerning is the role that betting companies play in preying on these individuals and causing the addictions in so many. The founder of the lobby group Clean Up Gambling, Matt Zarb-Cousin says this about the issues we are faced with in the BBC documentary Paul Merson: Football, Gambling and Me. Blame was laid at the door of betting firms who prey on vulnerable individuals with impulse control issues. Sixty per cent of betting company profits come from problem gamblers or those at risk of becoming problem gamblers. Destructive gamblers aren't, in other words, a tiny, tragic minority. They are the business model for an industry that has used technology to take gambling out of the high street and put it on everybody's smartphone.

In the documentary it is upsetting to see how helpless Merson feels towards his gambling addiction. In the documentary he talks about squandering the deposit for his house, which now meant he, his wife and three children without a permanent home and forced to continue to live in rented accommodation. This had left him crippled with self-hate. Which was what had encouraged Merson to quit. But he continued to struggle, admitting he found the repetitive nature of everyday life a chore. His biggest worry was whether he had the willpower to remain on the straight and narrow. "This is it," he said, his face crumpled in distress. "This is last chance saloon." Throughout the film he was honest enough to acknowledge the fact that he could likely relapse, and this would be another tragic tale in his battle against his addiction.

During the documentary Merson take's part in an experiment with researchers at the Imperial College London, with Dr Erritzoe. In the experiment he was presented with images of family life and beautiful natural scenery, Merson's grey matter stayed inert. However, when they changed the slide to a rolling dice or roulette wheel and it was fireworks. This made Merson then worried about how his brain would react to betting companies adverts. "I think the adverts are triggers," he says. "Now that I know more about how it can affect me, when the adverts come on, I turn them off." The 2005 Gambling Act (perhaps New Labour's worst domestic legislation) "allowed the links...to explode" through advertising. "Today it's almost impossible to watch a Premier League game without thinking about betting."

The 2005 Gambling Act can be seen as the modern incarnation of Gambling in Britain. This act led to the proliferation in gambling advertising and marketing. People started to become more familiar with betting adverts, such as Ray Winstone and Bet 365's adverts, that seemed to appear on every advert in the build-up to a match and at half-time as well giving the latest odds for in-play bets. However, what New Labour didn't anticipate is the development of smartphones and their capabilities. This and the boost in awareness of Gambling sites/companies through adverts and marketing have caused the explosion Merson talks about. People now have a bookie in their pocket and unlimited markets to bet on from Premier League football matches to Table Tennis. There has been mounting concern over the gambling industry's links with football. The stars who have promoted gambling firms include Alan Shearer, Robbie Savage, Jose Mourinho and Harry Redknapp and many others. But under new advertising rules to be introduced from October, gambling firms will no longer be permitted to use celebrities likely to appeal to under-18s

Former Scottish Conservative leader Ruth Davidson also looked at the relationship between football and gambling in a Channel 4 documentary. Davidson described the gambling industry's relationship with football as a "parasite that's taking over the host" in the Channel 4 programme. One of the more worrying findings from the documentary was the number of times we are exposed to gambling advertisements during a football match.

According to research by Dr Robin Ireland of the University of Glasgow, there were up to 716 gambling "exposures" in a match between Newcastle United and Wolverhampton Wanderers, both of whom at the time had gambling sponsors - equal to more than six logos per minute. The industries way of supposedly addressing the issues of problem gambling was to agree to a voluntary "whistle-to-whistle" ban on TV advertising during afternoon games. However, this doesn't consider the advertisements on pitch side hoardings or on team's shirts.

During the documentary John Whittingdale MP, was interviewed by Davidson. He is the junior minister overseeing the gambling review at the department for digital, culture, media, and sport (DCMS). Whittingdale admitted that online gambling has presented new public health concerns that should "trump" any fears about the impact on £3bn of annual betting duty revenue if industry profits are limited by stricter regulation. Any restrictions will be tough to put in place though, due to the amount of money involved and how unwelcomed it will be by the football authorities and betting groups. The gambling industry's annual contribution to football clubs' coffers of more than £100m – plus around £200m spent with broadcasters. While accepting these restrictions on advertising, the gambling industry has been campaigning against a possible crackdown of the sector in a government review. Since December 2020, ministers announced that they would be reviewing gambling laws, including sport sponsorship. But since this announcement the white paper into this has been delayed four times. The latest delay came it was said due to the resignation of Boris Johnson as prime minister, with nothing new announced yet regarding the white paper. The Observer also revealed in May 2022, how some of Britain's betting giants were quietly lobbying Treasury officials against an industry crackdown. The review was said to examine online stake limits, improved protection for online gamblers and gambling advertising. However, in regard to advertising, it is understood that ministers were considering a voluntary ban by football clubs, meaning not much would probably change in regard to this. Premier League clubs themselves were due to vote this summer on a ban on front-of-shirt sponsorship, but it was postponed. Premier League chief executive Richard Masters has blamed the "political hiatus" for the delay. But even if it was agreed by clubs to voluntarily agree to the ban on sponsorship, it would still only be phased in, meaning an immediate change wouldn't be forthcoming. Carolyn Harris, chair of the all-party parliamentary group for gambling related harm, said: "The stalling of the white paper has emboldened the gambling companies to seek new deals with football clubs. It's opportunistic of the gambling companies, who know the writing is on the wall. I'm disappointed because we're talking about a problem which is taking people's lives."

This has allowed three Premier League clubs, Everton, Fulham and Bournemouth, to agree new shirt deals with betting operators for the 2022-23 season. This means that eight of England's top football clubs have front-of-shirt gambling sponsors, while others have separate deals for sleeve sponsorship, logos on training kits and stadium advertising. Everton's new deal with the casino and sports betting platform Stake.com, is said to be a "club-record deal". It has been reported the deal is worth more than £10m a year and will run until at least the end of the 2024-25 season. Stake's global ambassadors include Canadian rapper Drake and the Manchester City striker Sergio Agüero. Drake is quite prominent in his promotion of the company as he bets astronomical fees on a range of sports including MMA and the UFC. A recent one saw him stake $2,296,211.30 on the scouse duo Molly McCann and Paddy "The Baddy" Pimblett both to win at UFC London. Both did this winning the rapper, $3,723,0777. In return for their part in winning him his bet he gave the scousers both Rolex's to say thanks. The absurdity of the stake and using the likeness of two high-profile fighters gave the company ultimate exposure. On other occasions he has bet similar amounts but not won, but ultimately, he isn't betting his own money, just promoting the company in his role as ambassador and giving it the ultimate exposure with crazy stakes that will grab the attention of the whole of social media. Bournemouth also unveiled its deal with global betting brand Dafabet in June. It said the deal would provide "crucial revenue". Fulham announced its sponsorship deal with W88 last month. The club said: "Presence on the shirt will allow the W88 brand to benefit from the global exposure of the Premier League, broadcast to a worldwide audience of over 3 billion people." The five other clubs with shirt sponsorship deals are Brentford (Hollywoodbets), Leeds United (SBOTOP), Newcastle United (Fun88), Southampton (Sportsbet.io) and West Ham United (Betway).

Recently West Ham's main sponsors Betway ended up in the news after being fined more than £400,000 for advertising on pages of the club's website targeted at children. It was discovered by the Gambling Commission that Betway's logo, which linked to the bookies' website, appeared on a section offering a chance to print a picture of a teddy bear for children to colour in. The Commission's regulations also state that responsibility for where logos appear lies with betting companies, such as Betway, resulting in them receiving the £408,915 fine rather than West Ham. A West Ham spokesperson said: 'The Betway logo appeared on a web page on the West Ham United website containing content that was targeted at Under 18s. Upon identification, it was immediately removed.' West Ham had before this also removed the sponsor from the shirt of Bubbles the mascot in the London Stadium on matchdays. The company have also been fined by the same commission two years ago. This was a UK record £11.6million for 'systemic historical failings' in tackling money laundering and problem gambling. As part of this, they were said to have failed to carry out effective social responsibility checks with a customer who deposited and lost £187,000 over two days.

This sponsorship though is not just restricted to the Premier League. If you look at the Championship and League One and you'd have discovered that another sixteen clubs had the same sort of deals in place. A decent amount of those without a shirt sponsorship deal would still have had a partnership of some sort with a betting company, normally coming under the banner of them being a 'principal partner'. Families who lost loved ones to gambling addiction have reacted with anger to the delay in the release of the Government's white papers, allowing the sponsorship exposure to grow. In a Daily Mail article released just after the announcement of the three new deals. Annie Ashton, from Leicester, whose husband, Luke, took his life in April last year after he started gambling during lockdown, said: "Football is a way into gambling addiction for so many people. It's shocking that clubs continue to blatantly ignore that." Charles Ritchie, co-founder of the charity Gambling with Lives, which supports and campaigns for families affected by gambling-related suicide, said: "We need an end to all gambling advertising. The delays to the white paper are disgraceful." James Grimes, who fronts the Big Step campaign striving to rid football of gambling advertising, said: 'This shows again that the Government must end all gambling sponsorship in football. By continuing to promote gambling, clubs are risking the health and lives of young fans.' A spokesperson for the Department for Digital, Culture, Media and Sport said: "We are undertaking the most comprehensive review of gambling laws in fifteen years to ensure they are fit for the digital age. As we have said all along, we will be publishing a white paper as part of a review of gambling legislation." But all you need to hear to see how serious the companies are taking it is their response to the potential dangers of gambling. A spokesperson for the Betting and Gaming Council, which represents some of the UK's biggest betting firms, said: "The regulated betting and gaming industry provides some of the country's most popular sport with vital funding, including the English Football League, which receives £40m. The government has previously stated research did not establish a causal link between exposure to advertising and the development of problem gambling." This being the one study conducted in Liverpool university mentioned previously. This however is completely undone by the findings from Paul Merson's documentary when his brain went 'Haywire' when faced with images of gambling.

Ultimately, the government need to publish their findings with more research conducted. Personally, I believe the adverts do trigger you to go to a website and check the latest odds on a game. That may just be me personally, but I believe there will be lots more like myself. Although I don't agree with the companies regarding the supposed 'casual links' they believe advertising has with problem gambling. The money they provide has developed football in the country. Due to the increased income to Premier League sides, alongside the TV revenue, allows sides to buy the very best talent, thus making it an even more appealing product to fans across the world. This doesn't bother me, as there is enough money from the owners themselves and other revenues to do this. What is more beneficial though is the money is trickling down into the lower leagues. The Premier League has put in well over £300million into grassroots football via the Football Foundation over the past two decades, while there's plenty more individual clubs put into the likes of local communities and supporting non-league clubs. Does this soften the blow, no, not at all, but it is a slight positive out of a wholly negative thing for the public. But when you consider the profit of £14.2 billion made by betting companies alone in 2020, £300million over the past two decades is nothing. However, another of our trusted spokespeople for the Betting & Gaming Council (BGC) trade body highlighted the industry's economic contribution. "BGC members support 119,000 jobs, generate £4.5bn in tax to pay for vital public services and contribute £7.7bn to the economy in gross value added," they said. "Betting shops alone employ around 46,000 people across the country, pay £1bn in tax to the Treasury as well as £60m in business rates for local councils, while casinos employ 11,000 staff and pay £500m a year in tax. These facts may be inconvenient for anti-gambling prohibitionists, but they demonstrate the huge economic contribution our members make to the country, which will be so important as we emerge from the pandemic."

Once again, the Betting & Gaming Council always have an answer to put a positive spin on how their greed for money is positive for the country and not negative. I'm 100 percent against these companies if you haven't already realised, but if anyone was still unsure which side to select the following information would make the most heartless of people realise how 'Evil' these companies really are. During Merson's documentary the most shocking finding was how betting companies (ab)use data harvested from their customers. "60% of the industry's profits come from people like us," Zarb-Cousin noted. "People who are…or are at risk of becoming addicted. It's not in their interests to reduce addiction." He then showed Merson the data harvested on someone he knew, by an un-named company, which gave them a life story. Of course, "they knew he was a gambling addict" and "know the (customers) who are addicted and the one's that aren't. But they are using the data that they could be using to prevent harm, to make it worse." Merson termed it "pure evil." Research suggests the small number of problem gamblers may be at increased risk. Last year, the House of Lords found 60% of gambling companies' profits came from the 5% of their users who are already problem gamblers or are at risk of becoming so. A data scientist who has worked for gambling firms, and spoke to Channel 4 anonymously, said: "The real money is if you able to make those customers bet on casino as well. In sports you can win if you're well-informed or know how to bet but in gaming, in the long run, you'll always be losing." He said gambling firms were using algorithms to identify customers who they might want to entice to bet more or try other products, deploying controversial incentives such as free bets and bonuses. "If you see someone is spending a lot, you'll want to make sure they're doing it regularly," he said.

 William Hill claimed to "promote important safer gambling initiatives like deposit limits," Merson noted that while "these companies say, 'set your limit,' you don't set your limit if you're a compulsive gambler." Merson is correct in this. I have 3 gambling accounts, setup at different times to benefit from new account bonuses. On all three of these accounts, I have set deposit limits. However, all these deposit limits can be changed within 24 hours, some even instantly. Another thing I found with Bet365 is that you must set a minimum deposit limit of £5. So, this can't be say £1, you still have to bet £5 a week. There is obviously cooling off periods or self-exclusions, which are different but to say deposit limits will stop someone who has serious gambling issues is farcical, when it is self-imposed and so easy to change.

What could also cause even bigger issues to gambling in the UK is changes that have occurred to US Gambling. In 2018, the US supreme court allowed gambling to become legal in all states. Since the Supreme Court's ruling, Americans have wagered more than $125 billion on sports. In essence, the "gamblification" of sports in the US would shock a UK bettor. "What has happened in the States since 2018, has, in so many ways, been a 'Hold my beer' moment," says Darragh McGee, an assistant professor in the Department of Health at the University of Bath who has examined the impact of online sports gambling on young adult males in the UK. "Gambling stateside has already accelerated far beyond what we would consider acceptable here in the UK."

These differences range from subtle to overt. In the former camp, take online payments: The UK has banned using credit cards for online gambling; US states (and UK bookmakers, who have pitched up stateside to take advantage of the laxer regulations) are busily expanding their use. The knock-on effect is now that other sports are looking to benefit from a relationship with gambling brands. The major US sports are a prime example of this. The NBA announced a new betting partner earlier this year, and the likes of the NHL and MLB have also struck similar deals over the last 12 months or so. For football, they continue to be a trailblazer in working with the industries. The FA Cup's deal with a bookmaker to live stream games is something that the likes of the Premier League might look to follow in some capacity, while we may see entire betting platforms starting to be integrated into a club's website or stream. This may see more American betting companies spring up, as they try to grab some of the huge amounts of money available and look to Premier League teams to promote their companies. Meaning advertisement will continue to grow and grow, meaning gambling exposure and issues related to gambling will accelerate even more.

6.1% of sportsmen would be classed as problem gamblers as stated at the start of this chapter. Some players have been very honest with how much of their earnings this has cost them.

Former Sunderland forward Michael Chopra hit the headlines with his gambling addiction after revealing losses of around £2 million in 2011." I reckon I've lost 70% what I've earned," is the estimated figure that former Spurs and brief Liverpool defender Stephen Caulker believes he lost gambling. "Football was my escape as a kid but that changed when I was chucked into the first team as a teenager and suddenly football came with pressure. My way of dealing with it, even in the early stages of my career, was gambling. I'm an addict. I'm addicted to winning, which people say is a positive in football but certainly not when it extends to gambling. I was addicted to trying to beat the system, because you convince yourself there is a system to it and you can beat it. You can never get your head around why you aren't." Caulker has spent various stints in the Sporting Chance clinic, his gambling led him to issues with his drinking too. "Being dropped rattled me even more because football was what I had relied on to make me feel better. So then the gambling was every single day. The pain of losing all my money, combined with the shame and guilt, ate away at me. So I'd drink myself into oblivion." Even after a warning from Spurs chairman about how his career was going, did nothing to stop him and his issues of the field didn't just cost him money earned but also potentially the heights his career could've reached. "I'd had one last gamble and lost a hell of a lot of money. A last blowout. It was at that point I finally accepted I could not win; that there was no quick fix, no more daydreaming I could save the world through one good night on the roulette wheel. It was all a fantasy that took me away from having to feel anything. I contemplated suicide a lot in that period. A dark time. Everything I'd gone through in football, where had it taken me?" This is the effect that gambling has on a professional footballer, something most young boys dream of as a child, that wasn't enough as this cruel addiction took over Caulker's life. There are many more players who have lost everything gambling throughout their

160

career. Former PFA Chairman Gordon Taylor, suggested that as many as 20 per cent of Premier League players are declared bankrupt within five years of retirement. Gambling isn't the sole cause of this but in some cases it has played a huge role.

What is as costly to players as money, is portions of their careers when they can't play football. Gambling has caused many to be banned for parts of their career. Two such players, were banned for what was said to be 'insider' information on transfer bettings. 'Lump on if you want' was the infamous WhatsApp message which ultimately saw England international Kieran Trippier banned for breaching FA betting rules. Trippier's friends took his advice literally and staked multiple bets on the move. A full FA investigation took place, and Trippier was eventually banned from all football-related activity for 10 weeks, fined £70,000 and forced to pay costs. All this was in relation to his move to Atletico Madrid and seen this ban upheld even in Spain. It was even proven Trippier didn't profit from this himself. Daniel Sturridge was also the victim of this, in 2019 he was found guilty of breaching the betting rules after allegations that he passed inside information over a potential transfer in January 2018. Originally, it appeared as though Sturridge was going to be handed a six-week ban with four of these weeks suspended, although the FA then appealed against the findings of an independent commission and decided thereafter to impose a four-month ban which applies to playing professional football for any club. This meant he was then sacked by his club at the time Turkish club Trabzonspor and fined £150,000. Sturridge lays the blame at the door of betting companies, who allow customers to bet on transfer activity.

This was also supported by the press, who asked for an end to all transfer betting markets. I second this as I am sick of texts off people claiming to know somebody who knows somebody and

161

who they're signing for or what club they're going to manage, all for them never to come in. Joey Barton is another high-profile football player who fell afoul of breaching the FA betting rules. The evidence stacked up against him considering it was revealed that he placed 1,260 bets over a period of ten years, including several wagers that related to his various team-mates. In April 2017, the FA decided to ban Barton for 18 months after considering a suitable punishment for his misdemeanours. The current Bristol Rovers manager admitted that he had held a registered Betfair account since 2004 and placed over 15,000 across a range of sports, with an average stake size of £150. Andros Townsend is another ex-England international who was caught breaking the betting rules by the Football Association after a bad habit spiralled out of control while on loan at Birmingham City. During the 2012/13 season, Townsend revealed that he lost £46,000 in one night amid a gambling addiction, with the ex-Tottenham player getting suspended for four months for breaching the betting regulations. The player revealed that his online betting started when he saw an advert on television and downloaded a bookmaker app. Yet another example of a player with a lot of money and spare time on his hands.

Reading up on the research I've come to realise that I probably bet more than I should do, but this is probably due to the normality of this. I have realised that I am very fortunate, as when I was researching for the book, I looked on my online accounts to see my Profit/Loss. The alarms for some would be that I did this on three separate bookmakers, this is due to new customer bonuses that enticed me to start accounts, but obviously this has served its purpose as I have kept the accounts. I am fortunate though because I am in profit on all accounts. Why? Pure Luck!!! I have had a few big winners that have got me out of the red, without these it would probably make bleaker viewing. What reading up on this whole chapter has done though has made me realise slightly that I need to slow down at the pace at which I was betting. Because although some people tell me I'm good at betting, that's not true, nothing is a cert in betting, and I've got extremely lucky. I've put limits on all my accounts to ensure I never lose too much, but I am fortunate unlike Merson in that I hopefully will not try to get round these. Unfortunately, I've seen how it has affected a few friends of mine and still does to this day, for me the saving grace was that I was never betting on betting terminals, because I have seen friends lose hundreds on this. But the thing that has struck me most when reflecting on the issues with gambling is why people do it.

When my Dad died and from when I have looked at my betting accounts, the most active time I had betting was just after his death. Betting was a way of me attempting to numb the pain I was feeling, something I have only realised now. During this time, I had a couple of big wins, and instead of stopping I continued to chase more wins, this is how gambling gets you. Did it help me to get over my dad's death? No, it left me delusional thinking somehow, he was looking over me and that's why I was winning. No that was pure luck, how else do you get two 100/1 bet builders in, in one month. Or win £1200 off a fiver on a UFC accumulator. It was all pure luck that could've been changed if one person in these bets got injured in the first minute. Even those wins have not helped me to overcome the depression and depths of despair I have felt since he died. Nothing will fill that void and alcohol and gambling are not going to help my mental health in anyway shape or form. Gambling to me is as dangerous an addiction as any. It scares me how easy it can be to fall into the traps of these companies, but worst of all how football and the government are facilitating it. I don't think I am a problem gambler, but what this chapter has helped me to realise is that although I may not have a 'problem', I need to be much more aware of the frequency of how much I bet, and hopefully anybody reading this who feels they may be in a worse position than me that this can help them to stop or seek help. Gambling is not good in any way shape or form, this is something I now realise, the buzz of winning doesn't last that long before you're losing money again.

7

Ownership

"This league is in danger of becoming one of the most boring but great leagues in the world"

Kevin Keegan in 2008 when Newcastle manager

Keegan would go on to say that the top four that year would be the same the year after. He would be correct, the so called 'Top 4' of Manchester United, Liverpool, Arsenal and Chelsea, would in fact be the same top 4 in the Premier League every season from 2005/6 to 2008/9. Keegan talked about how he felt it would be nearly impossible to break into what he described as the two separate leagues within the Premier League. "We're a million miles away from challenging for the league but if my owner backs me, we want to try and finish fifth and top the other mini-league."

Spurs entered the fray in 2010 finishing in the top 4 for the first time, but more important that season was the emergence of Manchester City who finished 5th that season, at that point their highest ever finish in the Premier League. There came the newly formed 'Top 6'. Since that point the top 4 league positions have rotated between the so called 'top 6' further emphasising Keegan's point back in 2008. The one sole anomaly to that was in 2015/16, when Leicester defied massive odds of 5000-1 to pull off probably the biggest surprise in footballing history to not only finish in the top 4 but win the league. Normality was resumed the season after though as Leicester finished 12th in the league and the top 6 in the league was reset with the 'big boys' again. In the last 20 years in fact the only two other teams along with Leicester to finish in the top 4 are Newcastle in 2002/3 and Everton in 2005/6.

The TV deal for the PL shows the gulf in income available to PL clubs compared to its European peers. In 2018/19, pre-pandemic, the deal for the rights to the PL was €3.8bn. When you compare this to €1.8bn for La Liga and €1.5bn for Bundesliga, to you see the gulf in money at the disposal of PL clubs. If you combine the TV deals for the PL's two nearest rivals, it still comes up short by €500m. The TV deal is said to balance out the financial strength of all the PL teams as the income is shared equally, but this is only true of the income from the TV rights sold in the UK to Sky and BT sports. The European TV rights for the PL, which aren't split in the same way, over five seasons up to and including the 2018/19 season accounted for 26% of the 'top 6' teams in the PL's income. The UK rights that where shared equally between all the league, only accounts for 51% of the total income to the league.

This is less than a quarter of the revenue generated created by the seven clubs in European competition that year. For example, Liverpool earned £52m more than Huddersfield in 2018/19. Clubs have no say in this either as all negotiations for TV rights are done by the PL themselves. Another factor that makes it very difficult for clubs to break the hold the 'top 6' have over the league is the commercial power these clubs have. Looking at Manchester City's income in 2018/19, 42% of their income came from commercial deals and TV accounted for 47% of their income that year. Huddersfield on the other hand, received 88% of their income through TV rights, 8% through commercial deals and 4% from match day income. Clubs outside of the big six, cannot compete with the clubs commercially and it widens the gap between the clubs. These clubs have higher profiles, which mean they can attract higher match day incomes through higher ticket pricing and are also able to gain more valuable sponsorships and commercial deals. Therefore, so many clubs find it difficult to break into the 'top 6' and when ownership is then factored in also, show the gap widening even more. Qualifying for the CL plays in a big part in the 'top 6's' income for each year and is why it is so important they finish in the top 4 each season. For example, if Manchester United fail to qualify for CL for 2 seasons consecutive their adidas sponsorship falls by £21m, which fortunately for them, hasn't happened since signing the deal, as they have only missed qualifying for one season before returning. However, even if that was to happen, they can still generate through other commercial deals, for example in 2021 they signed a £235m deal with TeamViewer to become their principal shirt sponsors. Clubs outside of the big six cannot sustain this and is why when Leicester and Everton did briefly qualify for the CL, were not able to sustain these positions, as the other clubs reinvested to insure, they retook their place.

In the same interview with the Guardian in 2008, where Keegan asked his owner Mike Ashley to 'back him' to win the 'mini-league', he insisted that he enjoyed an excellent relationship with Mike Ashley, Newcastle's owner, but then revealed that they are hardly in constant communication. "I get on great with the owner because I never talk to him." The comment about not talking to him, being a positive of the relationship may have been a premonition for how his relationship with Ashely would end. Newcastle would be relegated the following season in 2008/9. Keegan would leave at the start of that campaign due to issues with the owner and the club hierarchy, regarding the club's transfer policy, "It's my opinion that a manager must have the right to manage and that clubs should not impose upon any manager any player that he does not want." Keegan leaving would cause the fracture of relations between the owner and its loyal fan base.

Back in 2007-08 fans delighted to see the back of Newcastle's former owners – Sir John Hall and Freddy Shepherd – eagerly embraced 43-year-old retailer who not only bought them pints in the city's infamous Bigg Market but also frequented the local nightclubs. Ashley made trips to Blu Bamboo and Buffalo Joe's – and even took an excursion to an away game in a white van shared with fans. Further adhering himself to the fans he brought back the 'messiah' Keegan as manager after sacking Sam Allardyce. The feel-good factor for Keegan would soon be over though, as Dennis Wise was inexplicably appointed as executive director (football) but didn't connect well with Keegan at all. Once Derek Llambias switched from running the owner's favourite London casino to becoming Newcastle CEO, the manager was now fully isolated. The straw that broke the camel's back was when Wise told Keegan Newcastle were buying Xisco, an unknown Spanish striker, Keegan responded by walking out, claiming constructive dismissal and winning £2m at an employment tribunal.

Keegan wasn't wrong with his assumptions about Xisco, who would only make 9 appearances between 2008-2013, scoring one goal, he would have double the loan spells during his time at Newcastle than goals he scored. Suddenly Ashley no longer ventured into Newcastle city centre and rarely attended St James' Park. Supporters who believed Keegan could do no wrong, felt betrayed. On the day Joe Kinnear was controversially extracted from retirement and named as Keegan's shock replacement, the writing was surely on the wall for Newcastle in the 2008/9 season. This a man who it was never known whether unintentional or meant as a personal slight would call his French midfielder Charles N'Zogbia, as "Charles Insomnia", in TV interviews. He must have been a PR disaster for the HR department, he was out of his depths and stuck in the ways of the 'crazy gang' culture he once helped to shape at Wimbledon in the early 90s. The writing should've been on the wall from his first press conference. Whoever advised Ashley on the decision either secretly wanted to see Ashley fail or didn't have a clue about football. The most old school of managers launched into a tirade at his first press conference, swearing at local journalists not just once but 52 times. Things remained surreal until Kinnear required major heart surgery and, with Newcastle facing relegation, another Newcastle legend, Alan Shearer was appointed for the final eight games of the 2008-09 season. The announcement was made on April fool's day and although some thought it may be a hoax due to Shearer's lack of coaching experience, Ashley hoped for the feel-good factor of a club legend returning, would restore the fan support and pull them to safety. Unfortunately, even a legend motivating the fan base could not motivate a talented yet disengaged squad in which Michael Owen and Mark Viduka ranked among those who appeared to have checked out mentally of the club.

Relegation was sealed on the last day against Aston Villa. Shearer felt he could bring the club back to the premier league and began a rebuilding fling plan for how they could achieve that. But once again, Ashley who had now lost the support of the fans, further antagonised them more by freezing him out, never responding to the plans. Soon it became apparent his short-term contract would not be extended – and it was hardly startling when the popular Shearer's bar behind the Gallowgate End was renamed Nine. They would return to the PL the following season under Chris Hughton before then replacing him with Alan Pardew. They would finally achieve what Keegan had set out to do in 2008 by winning the 'mini-league', in 2011/12 finishing 5th. Pardew was named manager of the year by the LMA for the achievement. He was also rewarded with an unheard of 8-year contract by Ashley 5 months after the 5th place finish as well as his backroom staff. A Newcastle statement at the time announcing the deals said, "The club has awarded the long-term contracts to ensure it has the stability necessary to achieve consistent success in the Premier League and European club competition." Ashley responding to this breakthrough season by refusing to allow even a penny of net spend on the squad in the 2012 summer window to help 'achieve consistent success in the Premier League and European club competition.' Instead, Newcastle only reached PL safety when winning their very final away game in May 2013 at QPR. Pardew was also quoted at the end of the season as saying, "Thank God we're not in the Europa League again."

It brings into question how much clubs outside the 'top 6' want to play in the less prestigious European competition, and if they don't want to, whether that be due to the toll it takes on their squad, is their aim just to stay in the PL each year. Is this enough for loyal supporters? If the aim is not to be successful but is to avoid the drop.   The addition of the Europa Conference League must also affect the ambitions of the 'mini-league'. This also applies to their desire ti win cups, as surely, they don't want to win domestic cups then as it would also see them qualify for the Europa League too.

Newcastle, Pardew and Ashley would not need to concern themselves with this anyway as they wouldn't reach those heights again. Ashley went some way to then ruining the progress he had made with the supporters after their successful 11/12 campaign through some more questionable decisions. The first being his decision to change the name of the stadium synonymous with Newcastle 'St James' Park' to the 'Sports Direct Arena'. You could understand clubs seeking further sponsorship by selling the naming rights to their ground, but when it is the owners own company it defies the point of seeking extra funding. Therefore, it has been done out of his own personal interests and to raise awareness of his own company. He then also subsequently signed a highly contentious shirt sponsorship with the payday lender Wonga. The moral compass of Ashley comes into question, when he is openly allowing a company to promote themselves on his shirts, who pry on the weak, who are at rock bottom financially and get themselves deeper into a hole they will more than likely struggle to escape. When the company collapsed in 2018, with an estimated 200,000 customers still owing more than £400m in short-term loans. Allowing an online money lender to promote their business to a wide audience could potentially be seen as worse than using a gambling company. In 2014, the Financial Conduct Authority (FCA) found it had lent money to many who would never be able to repay, prompting a crackdown on the sector. Administrators have since received 380,000 eligible claims against the business worth £460m in total - an average of £1,200 a claim.

Kinnear reappeared as director of football. Tellingly, Pardew responded to a question about how he was coping in this structure by making vigorous chopping motions with his hands. The decision on the rebranding the stadium and shirt sponsorships can be seen as solely business minded reasons without concern for the fan's views, but the Kinnear decision is just baffling. He had been out of football for a long time and wasn't up to the modern way of thinking so what could he bring to the club and why did Ashley trust him so much. Whatever Ashley's reasons, Kinnear's return would bring some comedy gold for those, who weren't Newcastle fans and even then, I think some of the stories you would struggle not to see the funny side. Following his surprise appointment as director of football, Kinnear delivered a live radio interview in which he described Hatem Ben Afra as "Ben Afri", Shola Ameobi as "Amamobi", Yohan Cabaye as "Yohan Kebab" and Derek Llambias as "Derek LLambeezee". So maybe the "Insomnia" slips ups from the past were a genuine mistake. In his same interview where he was unable to remember his own players names, he was also found a bit wanting on some stats. He claimed to have made more than 400 appearances for Spurs (it was 258), signed Dean Holdsworth for £50,000 (it was £720,000) and won three Manager of the Year awards (he was LMA Manager of the Year once in 1994). Part of his role as director of football was to scout for potential new recruits. Sent out to scout for prospective signings, Kinnear thought he had unearthed a potential gem when he watched Birmingham City play in a Capital One Cup tie against Swansea. After the game, Kinnear told a Birmingham official he was interested in their left-back Shane Ferguson. The only problem? Ferguson was on loan at St Andrew's from Newcastle.

The final blunder came in January 2014, having been dissuaded from giving live interviews in order to prevent further embarrassment, Kinnear provided Sky Sports News with some quotes they could use on air. "No one will be leaving Newcastle during this transfer window," he said. Less than a fortnight later, and Cabaye joined Paris St Germain for £20m. Kinnear eventually resigned but by late December 2014, Pardew had endured enough and turned the tables on Ashley by defecting to Crystal Palace. Newcastle would be relegated again in 2015/16 before returning after one season out of under the tutelage of Champions League winning manager Rafa Benitez. Their first season back would see their highest finish in the Premier League to date finishing 10th in 2017/18 since the 2011/12 season under Pardew.

Ashley had openly been trying to sell the club since 2008 and never really took them down, as at least seven mooted buyouts failed. There has been local property developer Barry Moat, the mysterious Nigerian consortium, the Indian group fronted by Steve McMahon, the businessman Geoff Sheard (subsequently declared bankrupt), Amanda Staveley's first, forlorn, 2017 attempt, the mainly American collective led by Peter Kenyon and Dubai's Bin Zayed Group of those made public to the media.

The £300m takeover of Newcastle United was officially completed, in October 2021 with a Saudi-led consortium ending Mike Ashley's 14-year ownership of the club.
The Premier League confirmed the takeover in a statement on Thursday, saying it had received "legally binding assurances" that the Kingdom of Saudi Arabia will not control Newcastle United. Premier League officials found out how persistent he was to sell, with Richard Masters and his fellow executives believing wrongly Ashley would throw in the towel when confronted by their initial opposition to Newcastle's Saudi-led takeover, they soon learned that represented a serious underestimation of the billionaire. After 17 months of often highly nuanced, extremely technical, legal skirmishing Ashely would succeed in selling the club.

Only now with the backing of the Saudi led consortium may Newcastle have a chance of finally breaking the stranglehold the 'Top 6' have over the PL. As of 2022 Ashley's net worth is £3.73b, making him the 596th richest man in the world by Forbes estimation. This includes the money from the sale of Newcastle and Sports Direct becoming a public limited company in 2007, with Ashley pocketing $1.7bn from the move. This shows that Ashley did have money to pump into Newcastle if he chose to try to break into the top 4 and Champions League qualification. Ashley however remained a shrewd businessman throughout his time as owner, looking to use the transfer business as a way of generating money for himself by signing young and cheap and looking to sell for profits. He only broke Newcastle's transfer record of £22.5m spent Michael Owen in 2005, in July 2019 with £40m spent on Joelinton.

The only other time he spent over Owen's 2005 fee was on Joe Willock for £25m in 2021. This however should not be a problem for the PCP capital partners, who are said to have nearly 100 times the net worth of Ashley, at £320bn and who are motivated to break into the 'big boys' league. This point was emphasised by Amanda Staveley who said, "Newcastle United deserves to be top of the Premier League. We want to get there. It will take time, but we will get there," says Staveley, the chief executive of PCP Capital Partners who is now a director on the Newcastle board. "We want to see it get those trophies, obviously. At top of the Premier League, in Europe, but to get trophies means patience, investment, time. We want everybody to work with us to build the club towards what it needs to be." As of November 2022, at the close of the PL, Newcastle finds themselves in uncharted territory of 3rd in the league, 4 points clear of Manchester United in 5th place.

This chapter is not a chapter dedicated to Ashley's ownership of Newcastle but will focus on how ownership in the PL has changed the football we watch today. There have been many reasons that the ownership landscape has changed in the PL in the last 20 years, but even before then ownership in English football has played a big role in the footballing landscape. Ownership in the PL is something that has interested me for a long time. My final university dissertation was related to the topic. For my final piece of work on my Sport Development with Business BA (hons),I produced **'A study to explore Liverpool Football Club fans perceptions of foreign ownership'**.

This was done way back in 2014 and didn't start of as a study into just Liverpool fan's perspectives at the time but obviously for anyone who has done a dissertation, this is a working title that will change over time. My first title was 'Is football a business or a sport?', as you will find from this chapter and probably from your own knowledge, what started as a sport, the most loved national sport, has turned into a lucrative business that produces huge sums of money. During my research for the project, it became clear that the two factors that changed the scope of football to the 'modern' football we have now become accustomed too is the creation of the PL and the change in ownership of football clubs. The title then changed to, 'A study to explore fans perceptions of foreign ownership,' but this obviously changed as I focussed more on what had happened to Liverpool and the issues, they had with foreign ownership prior to 2010 and the current owners Fenway Sports Group (FSG). I remember seeing a school friend out in town, who was studying the same course but was completing their course the year after mine, who asked if I could send them my dissertation for her to look at. The next time I saw them they were made up I'd helped but commented, "How did that get a first? It was sh**". To be honest she wasn't far wrong, I've read over it as part of the process of writing this book and hope to God you can see how my writing has improved. In my defence academic writing is a lot different, everything needs to be referenced and you aren't allowed to give your own opinion. Looking back now as well I wish I'd just created a questionnaire and not limited myself to interviewing Liverpool fans on their perspective. One so that I could see whether opinions differ based on the experience of different owners but most importantly, so I didn't have to spend hours and hours transcribing the interviews I did for my research project. My main research objectives looked at the changes to the PL and fan experience, both I'm going to look at how ownership, in particular foreign ownership has affected these.

Owners of football clubs in English football have historically had other interests in mind when purchasing football clubs. Directors of clubs in the past used the clubs as a way of raising awareness of businesses they were involved in. Early professional football in England represented was seen as a microcosm of larger business, local Victorian and Edwardian businessmen made profits out of their role as local football club directors. Even in early 20th century, due to increasing popularity within working classes, this attracted the interest of local businessman and politicians. These businessmen who had become involved in football by owning a football club, seen it as an opportunity to cash in on popular connections between working classes, leisure and sport. This shows that ownership of football clubs even in the early 20th century was with other interests in mind and not simply with the supporters of clubs in mind.

This business involvement in football continued into the late 20th century. In 1983 Tottenham became the first publicly traded football club. This led to most major share packages in football clubs being purchased by British business elites including Racehorse owners, heirs of fortunes, construction magnates. The first foreign owner involved in English football, was Mohamed Al Fayed (who bought Fulham in May 1997), his ownership was to expand his presence in English and London markets with marquee purchases of shops and property in the area (such as Harrods). At the time of completing my dissertation in 2013, this had risen to ten PL clubs being under foreign ownership in the 2013/14 season: Arsenal, Chelsea, Man United, Man City, Liverpool, Aston Villa, Southampton, Cardiff, Sunderland and Fulham. In the current 22/23 season 15 out of 20 club's majority shareholders are foreign. Out of the 5 clubs that are not under foreign ownership, Tottenham are the only 'Top Six' side with a British owner.

Other leagues have stricter ownership rules which make such scenarios impossible. In the Bungesliga, oft-cited as the model league for sustainable growth, sensible finances and organic fan-involvement, 51 percent of the club must be in the hands of the fans, so no external owner can have majority control. Ligue 1, meanwhile, has a body which evaluates potential sales, but like in the Premier League, this did not prevent many foreign investments, some with questionable intentions, taking over French clubs. Paris Saint-Germain, in a similar situation to City and Newcastle, are backed by the Qatari state. Bordeaux, Marseille (USA), Lille (Luxembourg), Nice (UK), Monaco (Russia) and Nantes (Poland) are all foreign owned in France. There is a heavy US presence in Serie A too (Genoa, Fiorentina, Milan, Spezia, Roma, Venezia), while Bologna (Canadian) and Inter (Chinese) are also foreign owned. Another difference between the PL and its European peers was the UK was the most open major developed economy, welcoming to individuals and finance from around the world.

With the value of TV rights spearing globalisation and the increasing number of international players boosting the PL international profile. Gambling and E-Gaming, presenting new opportunities a new wave of investors this time from abroad emerged little did we know at the time how significant this would be. When you compare the income of the PL to its nearest rivals, it is also clear to see why Owners have chosen to select the PL, rather than other leagues. Deloitte reported the total incomes for the PL in 2018/19 before the pandemic hitting, as a record night for the PL at £5.85bn. This was nearly £2.5bn more than La Liga, who racked in £3.38bn. In 3rd position, was Bundesliga, who earned £3.35bn. When you compare this £5.85bn to the global income and what it accounts for it doesn't seem massive, as this is

177

3% of the world economy. But this amount makes up 20% of the global football economy, which when compared to other businesses, is similar levels to Saudi Arabia's in the world market for oil. TV deals play a huge factor too and once again this sees the PL well out in front of its competitors. The deal for the PL is £3.8bn, whilst the combined figures of La Liga £1.8bn and Bundesliga £1.3bn cannot match this. Commercial deals in the PL account for £1.6bn, which is more than the TV rights of the Bundesliga, showing the huge potential that attracts foreign owners, to this huge potential windfall of cash.

Some of the original shareholders sold off their football assets and done so at substantial profits, showing that even before the influx of foreign owners into English football, British businessman saw football clubs as an investment opportunity. One such example of one of these business elites making money off their investment is In 2003, English businessmen Ken Bates who originally took over Chelsea FC for £1, sold the club for £140million to Russian billionaire Roman Abramovic, who became the second foreign owner in the PL. Chelsea's takeover by Russian Roman Abramovich was a watershed moment for English football and the game hasn't been the same since.

The legacy that Abramovich left as Chelsea owner cannot be discussed without alluding to the club's past before him. The Blues had not won the top-flight title since 1955 and had never lifted the European cup. Chelsea's only past silverware was the 1971 UEFA Cup Winners' Cup and three FA Cups between 1970 and 2000. Abramovich transformed them into serial winners and a founding member of the original 'top 4', which later became the 'top 6' due to his influence as a foreign owner. They won five Premier League titles, five FA Cups, three League Cups, two Champions Leagues, two Europa Leagues, two Community

Shields, one Super Cup and finally the Club World Cup, his investment and oversight helped turn them into a powerhouse of the modern game, shattering the status quo.

In his first transfer window he spent in excess of £100m. Spending heavily on recruits would become a recurring theme under Abramovich with star names a guarantee. Some of the big hitters in his first window were Claude Makelele and Hernan Crespo amongst others. Abramovich spent more than £2 billion on player signings and another £90 million on hiring and firing managers as a total 13 different men across 15 different managerial spells came and went, ripping up the conventional rulebook which suggested stability in the dugout was the foundation of a lasting dynasty.

When Abramovich originally decided to buy an English team in 2003, he and his advisers drew up a five-club shortlist: Manchester United, Tottenham, Chelsea, Arsenal and Liverpool. A source close to Abramovich at the time told ESPN that contact was made with Spurs chairman Daniel Levy, while Arsenal informed Abramovich they were not for sale. Liverpool was ruled out and United's asking price was thought to be too high at £500m, but Abramovich already had connections to London because he already owned property in Knightsbridge, one of the most expensive parts of London to live.

Abramovich had no specific affinity to Chelsea and how he come about his money was also a contentious issue. Most of his wealth was acquired from dividends and the sale of private assets from the break-up of the former Soviet Union. One of the firms he had co-founded was Sibneft, which is a subsidiary of Gasprom. This was a company of his that has come under scrutiny and one for which he was sued by a fellow oligarch Boris Berzovsky over, said that he claimed he was owed €5bn for ill-gotten sale of Sibneft, which they co-founded. Although Abramovich would win that case in 2012, Jonathan Sumption QC, acting for Abramovich, admitted that the process of auctioning Sibneft "was easy to rig and was in fact rigged." These and his deals that helped former Russia president Boris Yeltsin win reelection in 1996 before helping to keep his successor, Putin, in power, didn't raise eyebrows when he first took over Chelsea. From within the U.K. government or the Premier League at the time but would ultimately be the reason he was 'forced' to sell in 2022.

What most forget is that he may also never have taken over Chelsea, was it not for a victory at the end of the 2002/3 PL season. I remember the game vividly as I was in the pub watching it with my dad, a must win for Liverpool or Chelsea, that would decide, who finished in fourth place, had somehow fallen on the last day of the season. Then-chief executive Trevor Birch told the Chelsea team before their final game of the 2002-03 season that victory was essential to help the club avoid financial ruin. **Denmark winger** Jesper Gronkjaer scored the goal which secured a 2-1 win over Liverpool and assured Champions League qualification by finishing fourth. 9-year-old me was obviously aware of the importance of getting in the CL, something Liverpool had done the previous year. But maybe that loss made Abramovich make his final decision, with the riches of the CL guaranteed. Six weeks later, Abramovich bought the club for £140m and immediately began spending money on top players to close the gap on Manchester United and Arsenal. What felt like unlimited funds at that time, potentially could've been Liverpool's and the success Abramovic brought to Chelsea, may have seen them remain a mid-table team without. However, we can't be certain what his intentions were. "The Gronkjaer goal is probably the most important goal in the history of Chelsea," Kieran

Maguire, author of "The Price of Football", told ESPN. "Whether Abramovich would have bought the club without Champions League football is the question but that certainly helped seal the deal. The total spending in the Premier League in 2002-03 was £187m. In 2003-04, it doubled to £390m. It never dipped back down to those levels after. Abramovich was a contributory factor not only to the increase in player purchases, but it helped the acceleration of wages as well."

After the players came the manager. He sacked the manager he inherited in Claudio Ranieri and replaced him with 'The Special One', FC Porto's rising star Jose Mourinho. Mourinho brought the star factor off the pitch, that he had also spent millions during transfer windows buying for on it. Mourinho had won the UEFA Cup and CL in the previous two campaigns with his underdogs FC Porto and had shown already he could take on and defeat Manchester United. Mourinho won the title in his first two seasons, seizing on the wider disgruntlement at Chelsea's newfound wealth to create a fearless siege mentality that would form the bedrock of future successes.

A 2005 report from Deloitte analysing Abramovich's first full year at Chelsea stated the club's wage bill had skyrocketed 110% to £114.8m, a figure the firm claimed was "almost certainly" the highest in world football at the time. That same season, the other 19 top-flight English clubs combined spent less on player salaries than they did the previous year. "Abramovich showed that you could be a disruptor to the existing duopoly of United and Arsenal through spending money, investing in both managers and players," Maguire said. "And also, that could result in payback almost immediately because they started to win trophies. To a certain extent, that opened the eyes of other potential investors who saw the glamour of the Premier League and realised they could perhaps do similar."

What Abramovich also did was break the stranglehold that Manchester United and Arsenal had over the PL. In 2003, Manchester United and Arsenal had won 10 out of 11 titles between them since the Premier League's inception in 1992. The only other time this has been threatened was in 1995 when Blackburn Rovers won the league. Industrial businessman Jack Walker used the proceeds of selling his family's sheet metal business to buy his boyhood club, Blackburn Rovers, taking full control in 1991. Walker spent aggressively: Blackburn hired former Liverpool legend Kenny Dalglish as manager, earning promotion from the Second Division a year later before breaking the British transfer record to sign striker Alan Shearer for £3.6m. But that success did not last; Sadly, Walker died in 2000, his family gradually withdrew funding and the club fell down the divisions as low as League One before stabilising in the Championship, where they are today. Arsenal and United at the time were the flag bearers for the conventional style of ownership at the time, which worked well for them before Chelsea come along. They financed the club and investment in the squad through broadcast income, matchday revenue and commercial activity. Chelsea however completely changed this financial sensibility almost overnight. "Under Abramovich, Chelsea lost over £900,000-a-week every week for 19 years," Maguire said. "That disrupted the normal business model as before that, it was ticket sales, broadcasting - which was outside the control of individual clubs -and commercial deals. Suddenly you had benefactor owners coming in and pumping in from another source. What the likes of Abramovich did was they made the existing elite conscious that their broad monopoly could be challenged and there could be people not only coming into the Premier League itself but potentially if someone

182

came into Bilbao in Spain or Hamburg in Germany - that could take away the expectations that some clubs in those countries had about been trophy winners and qualifying for the Champions League, making progress every season."

Abramovich's effect on English football is seismic. He used the most aggressive form of financing a club to achieve success, that world football had ever seen up to that point. Others followed him and applied the same financial method, but it also forced others to reinvest their money differently. To stand any chance of sticking with Chelsea, clubs had to spend the money generated through broadcasting rights on better players. This in turn improved the star factor of the league, with the some of the best players plying their trade in the league. The new business model though saw at first the 'top 4' breakaway from the others, as they took the risky method of spending to achieve more money through CL qualification.

Seven years after Abramovich's arrival, UEFA approved the introduction of financial fair play, a system designed to block teams from taking a shortcut to Europe's top table, restricting wages as a percentage of expenditure and capping losses over a multiyear period. But by 2010, Sheikh Mansour had already bought Manchester City (2008) in an attempt to replicate Chelsea's progress, and the sheer scale of the Premier League's television income meant many clubs still enjoyed greater flexibility than their European rivals. Since the takeover in 2010, they have won 6 PL titles, their first title since 1967/68 season. They have effectively bought themselves a position at the top table and became the last member of the 'top 6'. They also narrowly lost in the CL final in 2020/21, the one trophy that has evaded them since the takeover. Besides Leicester, every club to have won the Premier League after Sheikh Mansour bought Manchester City in 2008 has spent more than £1billion since that day. And it comes as no surprise that the number of trophies won by each of those clubs descends in keeping with how much cash they've splashed. City have spent £1.8bn in this time. In that time Chelsea have spent £1.6bn, United £1.4bn and both Liverpool and Arsenal just over £1bn.

The league has worked hard at promoting its brand overseas, catering to a global audience of an estimated 1.35 billion viewers across 188 countries. The globalisation of the English game can also be seen on the pitch, as well as in the boardroom. According to The Times, this season the figure stands at 41.2 %, a 17 year high. The last time English players made up over 40 % of players in the PL - besides this season - was back in 2011/12. It was at its lowest in 2013/14 when English players made up just 34.2 % of the footy stars. Of the 'Big 5' leagues, the PL is only ahead of Serie A's, whose domestic player percentage stands at 39.3 %, while in the Bundesliga it is 45.2 percent, Ligue 1 boasts 47% and LaLiga Santander leads the way with 58.3 %. The globalisation of the footballers in English football isn't just restricted to the PL either. The levels of foreign players outside the topflight is surprisingly highly too: Championship (47%), League one (34%) and League two (24%). Across the 92 clubs in the football league, over 40% of footballers in England were not English. It is a similar situation on the touchline, too, with just four of the 20 Premier League coaches being English and none of those coach one of the Big Six.

The lasting effect of Abramovich's spending can still be seen today and rather than stopping has got 'worse'. Premier League clubs' gross transfer spend totalled £1.9bn in the summer 2022 window, the highest spend ever recorded in a single transfer window by a margin of £487.8m, according to Deloitte's Sports Business Group. The previous record was set in the 2017 summer transfer window, when clubs spent £1.4bn. In 2021, Premier League clubs spent £1.1bn during the summer window. With the January transfer window still to come, the 2022/23 season already has the highest transfer spend since the two-window season began (£1.92bn), narrowly ahead of 2017/18 (£1.86bn). Tim Bridge, lead partner in Deloitte's Sports Business Group, commented: "The record level of spending during this transfer window is a clear indication of Premier League clubs' confidence, as fans return to stadia and a new broadcast cycle begins. It's now become part and parcel of the Premier League that clubs are willing to pay significant sums to maximise performance. This season, the desire to acquire playing talent has reached new levels as the pressure for clubs to stay in the competition is higher than ever before."

New ownership acted as a catalyst for increased spending this summer. Chelsea spent more than any other Premier League club; £157.8m more than they did last summer (2022: £255.3m; 2021: £97.5m), and £53.3m more than the next biggest spenders (Manchester United: £202.0m). Abramovich's past links to the Russian government and his relationship with Putin, which prior to the Ukraine war had caused the British government and FA no issues, now made Abramovich, the bad egg they no longer wanted part of football. Abramovich did flirt with the idea through a failed attempt to pass "stewardship and care" of the Blues to Chelsea's trustees, meaning selling his beloved Chelsea was the only option. And, after a three-month process, a consortium led by Los Angeles Dodgers owner Todd Boehly has now completed a £4.25bn purchase of the club.

When you compare the spending across Europe's 'big five' leagues you can really see the effect that foreign ownership has had on the spending in the PL, ignited by Abramovich's methods towards transfers. Premier League clubs' gross spend (€2.2bn) stood at almost three times their closest peers' (Serie A: €749.2m), and more than four times their furthest (Bundesliga: €484.1m). Premier League clubs were responsible for 49% of spending across the 'big five', during the window, the highest proportion since summer 2008. Total grosses spend among the rest of the 'big five' this summer (€2.3bn) only narrowly surpassed that of the Premier League alone (€2.2bn) and was €0.9bn below the average for the three summer windows prior to the pandemic (2017-19 three-year average: €3.2bn). Of total Premier League spending this summer, 39% went to clubs in either La Liga, Serie A, the Bundesliga or Ligue 1 compared to a pre-COVID three-year average of 47%. Overall, 62% of Premier League spending went to clubs outside of the English system, with 17% received by Portugal's Primeira Liga and Holland's Eredivise, marking a record high. PL clubs look to sign the best players from other leagues and in doing so trying to strengthen their position as the 'top' league, is now the tried and tested method. Only three teams outside the PL really mimic the spending of PL teams in, PSG, Real Madrid and Barca. In doing so Barca are on the brink of financial ruin, as their fan owned model cannot sustain the finances needed to spend the money PL clubs are, with lower TV deals being another big factor.

Abramovich though was not just a nightmare for some of the giants outside the PL. It was also a nightmare approach for other owners in the PL and many of the foreign owners who followed him could not apply the same approach he did. He bankrolled the success. Abramovich's approach was in many senses a nightmare for other owners because he bankrolled success independently, absorbed short-term financial pain in the pursuit of success and, crucially, attended matches with a regularity not replicated by, say, the Kroenkes at Arsenal or the Glazer family at Manchester United. United's takeover was a leveraged buyout that loaded debt onto the club. When the Kroenkes bought out second majority shareholder Alisher Usmanov in 2018, they borrowed £557m to do so, although insisting at the time the club would not be responsible for the debt. The fact this didn't happen with Chelsea, not only allowed him to sell the club more easily, but also ensured he will have a good relationship with Chelsea fans, who love the man, who has spent his own money to bring success the club they love.

The Glazer family were the next foreign owners in the PL and they came in 2005, but would never get anywhere close to the relationship Abramovich shared with Chelsea supporters. The American owners started out on the wrong foot with their leveraged £790m takeover of United in 2005 and didn't do a whole lot right after that in the eyes of supporters. But the story of how the takeover came about slightly tarnishes the man who made United the team they were during the 90s and 00s, their most successful manager of all time and one of the most important names in British football, Sir Alex Ferguson. One of the reasons the Glazers were able to buy Manchester United, was due to an argument over a racehorse involving Fergie and major shareholders John/Susan Magnier and JP McManus. If this argument had never taken place, who knows whether they would've been able to takeover. The horse in question was called Rock of Gibraltar and was part-owned by Ferguson and Susan Magnier. During its career there was no issues. It was a star and won 10 of his 12 starts and accumulating £1,164,804 in prize money across two seasons.

However, upon its retirement, there was a dispute over the breeding rights of the horse. Ferguson believing his half-ownership of the horse entitled him to half of the breeding rights as well. Magnier and McManus, owners of Coolmore - the largest breeding operation in the world for thoroughbred racehorses - disagreed. On November 17, 2003, a statement issued on behalf of Magnier read: "Coolmore Stud has today been advised that legal proceedings have been initiated against Mr John Magnier by Sir Alex Ferguson alleging certain ownership rights to the stallion Rock of Gibraltar. If this legal dispute was taking a place in Ferguson's personal life it would probably raise eyebrows in the boardroom, but the fact he was suing major shareholders from the club was a completely different matter. In retaliation to airing their dirty laundry for all to see, in 2004, Magnier and McManus submitted their infamous list of 99 questions to the Old Trafford board attempting to gain information on the club's finances and transfer dealings. They even threatened to "take action" against United if they were not given satisfactory replies. The club had now been dragged into a war against two of its major shareholders and were being forced to support their manager, who was the backbone of the whole club, as has been seen since his departure in 2013.

Roy Keane, his captain at the time recalled this during the time in his book 'The Second Half'. "Somebody I met in Ireland had told me to tell him [Ferguson]: 'You are not going to win this.' I mentioned it to him," Keane wrote. "And I told him that I didn't think it was good for the club, for the manager in a legal dispute with shareholders. I felt I was entitled to say that. He was just a mascot for them. Walking around with this Rock of Gibraltar – 'Look at me, how big I am,' – and he didn't even own the bloody thing!" Magnier and McManus though, continued to work away behind the scenes and were now increasing their shares by buying shares from minor shareholders, through their company Cubic Expression. Whilst Ferguson was now pleading for calm and asking the United fans who had obviously backed him, to not go ahead with planned protests at the 2004 Cheltenham Festival against the shareholders. He said this, "The Cheltenham Festival is a classic meeting in the National Hunt racing calendar, which people from all over the world and all walks of life come to enjoy. It is effectively the equivalent of the FA Cup final to horse racing fans, and I would not wish this special festival to be marred in any way. I am therefore asking supporters to refrain from any form of protest and am strongly opposed to any violent, unlawful or disruptive behaviour which may reflect badly on the club and its supporters in general."

Through all the distractions caused by this very public argument, Malcolm Glazer, owner of the Tampa Bay Buccaneers NFL team, was keeping more than just a watchful eye on the situation. Since March 2003, much like Cubic Expression's, they had started buying up shares in United - starting off at 2.9% before rising to 3.17%, 8.93%, 15%, 16.31% 19% and close to 30% by October 2004. They then made an offer to Cubic Expression's in May 2005, one that was accepted and purchased the 28.7% stake owned by Magnier and McManus. The racehorse owners would possibly have sold anyway, but by actively seeking more shares themselves, displayed the business acumen the two 'horse experts' had, ensuring they maximised the money they could make off the deal. Within a month the Glazers, would acquire 98% of the clubs' shares signing off on a deal worth £780m.

What happened in the battle between Ferguson vs McManus/Magnier? Well Ferguson settled out of court in March 2004 for a one-off payment of £2.5m. This probably didn't feel such a bitter pill for Coolmore racing operation to take, considering they made over £200m in the sale of their shares to the Glazers. In his autobiography, released in 2013, Ferguson said this, "Rock of Gibraltar was a wonderful horse; he became the first in the northern hemisphere to win seven consecutive Group

1 races, beating Mill Reef's record. He ran in my colours under an agreement I had with the Coolmore racing operation in Ireland. My understanding was that I had a half-share in the ownership of the horse; theirs was that I would be entitled to half the prize money. But it was resolved. The matter was closed when we reached a settlement agreeing that there had been a misunderstanding on both sides. Obviously, there was a potential clash between my racing interests and the ownership of the club, and when a man stood up at the AGM and insisted that I resign, there was awkwardness for me. I have to say that at no point was I side-tracked from my duties as manager of Manchester United. I have an excellent family lawyer in Les Dalgarno, and he managed the process on my behalf. It didn't affect my love of racing and I am on good terms now with John Magnier, the leading figure at Coolmore."

None of this is probably a reassurance for United fans though, who have had to suffer with the reign of the Glazers. But we cannot say for sure that without the argument, that the shareholders wouldn't have sold anyway. However, being at war with the legendary manager of the club you own shares with, over something completely not football related, who has the backing of the fans and the board, probably made their position impossible. The fans supported him in his battle, but unfortunately Ferguson didn't support them in their battle against the owners, something that shocks me from the outside. The same could be said of players of the time, who now come out and openly criticise them, but didn't when on their payroll, which by the way I can understand in terms of wanting to just do your job and support your family. But this ownership now seems to be coming to an end but has been a disastrous relationship since day one and in no way similar to Chelsea's and Abramovich's.

The vast majority of United's fanbase probably rejoiced at the news they were planning to sell and are delighted to see the back of them. From the outside rival fans will claim that they have outspent most of their rivals with over £1bn paid out on transfers for players over the last 17 years. This argument though will fall on deaf ears, and there is no defence in United fans minds for the indefensible. The main grievances they air towards their owners from the takeover of their club, is the debt, the dividends, the state of the stadium and the lack of success, all this means there will never be a truce between fans and owners. Anti-Glazer sentiment reached unprecedented levels after the collapse of the European Super League in April 2021 with demonstrations inside and outside Old Trafford, even when the team are winning. One such protest caused the cancellation of United Vs Liverpool, which is one of the biggest games not just for both clubs, but sky and the tv market, who instead showed the carnage that ensued inside the stadium.

Looking at the finances at United, it is clear why the fans hate the owners so much, even going to the lengths of singing Songs about cutting up chairman Joel Glazer 'from head to toe' are commonplace. Swiss ramble, the football finance blogger broke down the club's official accounts and calculated that since taking over in 2005, the owners had cost the club £1.1bn. The total amount is £1.13bn broken down to this: £743m interest payments, £147m debt repayments, £166m dividends, £55m directors' remunerations and £23m management fees. During this time The Glazers have personally also pocketed £465m through numerous sales of shares over that period. From 2010-2021, United had interest payments of £517m, which were nearly as much as the rest of the PL combined (£536m). The Glazers have made no effort to lower the debt on the club, the gross debt stands at £636m- virtually unchanged from 2006 when the figure stood at £604m.

The songs about wanting the owners dead, doesn't bother them though, they're too far away to notice or care. Unlike Abramovich they aren't welcome at the ground they own and haven't been seen at Old Trafford in years. Instead, those linked to them in the UK are punished, protesters have managed to seek out executive vice-chairman Ed Woodward and his successor Richard Arnold and have targeted their homes. However, all the Glazers care about is money and if the sale of the club does go through, it's because they want to, not because they're being forced to. The £4.25billion sale of Chelsea and a rather pessimistic economic climate in the UK has suddenly made selling up sound like a very good idea. United's owners, like the FSG at Liverpool, have been tempted to test the market. The collapse of the Super League will also be a big factor (we will look at this in the next chapter).

The fan demographic at the club has changed lots since the takeover as well, with some loyal fans leaving to form their own non-league side FC United, whilst some still not able to give up on their beloved United, wear yellow and green scarves, dating back to the original days of the club as Newton Heath. Old Trafford as well, once the envy of all other clubs in England, has now fell behind most of its nearest rivals, and needs a serious makeover. They have appointed planners to look at the best option for the ground, whether that be improving the current stadium, knocking it down and building on the same site, or moving elsewhere. According to reports though, the Glazers if they were to stay would choose the cheap option of renovating what they already have, but even this isn't an easy option. Not only has the stadium fell into disrepair but so has Carrington there once lauded training base. Ferguson declared it as the best in the

PL, but now finds itself behind others in the PL. It isn't just the dodgy tiles in the swimming pool, mentioned by Ronaldo, that need sorting out. Millions more needs to be spent on upgrading Carrington, and plans that have been drawn up include the possibility of a club hotel on site for the players.

Ronaldo, in his hugely controversial interview with Piers Morgan, is one of the only players to speak out against the Glazers, when still playing for them. He said," The Glazers they don't care about the club. I mean, in professional sport, Manchester is a marketing club. They will get their money from the marketing- the sport, they don't really care in my opinion." Ronaldo is right in the fact that United's commercial income has increased by 500% since the Glazers took over in 2005, and they have done a very good job of sorting some of the largest marketing deals in the clubs' history. The five-year deal the signed with the German global technology company TeamViewer, was worth £235m, which is a PL record too. According to Deloitte's 2015 Annual Review of Football Finance, commercial revenue accounted for just 27% of revenue for all Premier League clubs. For Manchester United, that figure is 50%. That tells us the club is making considerably more of its global profile, and its global and regional sponsorship portfolios. This has continued and United are still ahead of all their nearest rivals still, the deal they signed with Adidas in July 2014, was said to be worth at least £750m over ten years. Once again though the question arises of where this money has gone to improve them as a team, although they have outspent rivals on transfers, this hasn't brought success on the pitch and is another grievance of the fans. Since Ferguson left in 2013, the club has won: 1 FA Cup (15/16), 1 Europa League (16/17), 1 Carabao Cup (16/17) and 1 Community Shield (16/17).

Prior to that, the club had won every cup available under the partnership between the Glazers and Ferguson, winning: 5 PL titles, 1 CL title, 1 World club title, 2 League cups and 1 FA Cup. Part of their failure to give the fans what they want in terms of what the fans see on the pitch and the success on it, is down to never find a long-term replacement for Ferguson. With 8 managers in 9 years, including temporary managers, with the longest reign and most successful in terms of PL finish (2nd) and Trophies (3), being 3 years under Jose Mourinho. Whatever happens next with the club though, nobody will be sad to see the Glazers go and that is a good starting point for any new owner. Whoever comes in will be seen as an improvement on the current owners, if they are prepared and make efforts to make the club debt-free and also inject money to make the club successful again. They will also need to learn from the Glazers' mistakes and build better relationships with fans. Something the Glazers' realised too late, setting up fans' advisory boards and promising a fan share scheme, but this was like sticking a plaster over a gunshot wound. The new owners also need to be visible and accessible, attending Old Trafford, rather than remaining in the US at their headquarters there. They also need to show the fans that it's not about the money (for them it obviously will be) but this can be done by letting the fans have more say in how the club is run. But like I've said the bar will not be set very high for any new owners-for the sole reason that they will have a huge head start, because they won't be the Glazers.

United were not the only fan base to turn on American owners and fight against owners, like they had never done in the past. This is what formed my dissertation to just focus on Liverpool fans opinions, something I knew at the time limited my research, but is also something I regret now as not much research has been done into the topic. The reason though was that it was so important to me to investigate the effect this had on fans and more importantly the team I love Liverpool FC. This was a very hard time for all Liverpool fans, one which caused fans to argue with each other about the best way to respond to what was going on off the pitch, but scarily a time when the club may nearly not have existed. Liverpool's current owners FSG come under fire from fans for supposed lack of spending, but what these fans sometimes forget is the sh**show they had to takeover and what they have achieved since then, was probably in some fans wildest dreams as they marched round Anfield before games asking for previous owners to leave or organising stay behinds at Anfield to have their opinions heard.

LFC was owned by the Moores family from the early 1960's, they were local businessmen, who had made their money from the Littlewoods Pools and mail order business and were a major and generally respected employer in Liverpool area. These shares would then be inherited by John's nephew David Moores in 1991, who became chairmen of the club, after inheriting part of the family fortune. Moores was chairman and majority shareholder for 16 years and was a lifelong fan of the club. All the choices he made he felt were for the best of the club and his love for the club was never in question. However, he realised he didn't have the money required to keep the reds at the top and restore them to their former glory. LFC historian John Williams said this about the reasons for David Moores deciding to sell the club in 2007 to two American businessmen George Gillett and Tom Hicks, *'certainly he did realize that he no longer had the finances, or local people no longer had the finances... and that Liverpool was now a club of such stature in this new era that you needed people with hundreds of millions, not tens of millions, to invest.'*
This was the knock-on effect of the arrival of Abramovich, which had completely changed the landscape of English football. Under

Moores helm the club had won the UEFA CL against all odds in 2005 and had also reached the CL final again the summer before the sale of the club, losing to AC Milan who they defeated in the 2005 final, losing 2-1 in Athens 2007. However, now with billionaires entering the fray, Moores was a pauper in comparison, and he knew Liverpool were in danger of being cast adrift from their big spending rivals. Even before the CL win in 2005, he had decided to sell the club, as he was convinced the club needed a new ground to compete and knew he couldn't fund it himself. He also couldn't compete with the spending power in the transfer market and knew that on paper the team had been performing better in Europe than they should've, however league positions had fluctuated and finishing top 4 wasn't a guarantee.

After the decision was made, it was then up to chief executive Ricky Parry and Moores to find the best suit for Liverpool, something that would be a long-drawn-out process from the original decision in 2004 to sell. However, this looked to be coming to an end in December 2006, when an exclusivity agreement was struck with Dubai International Capital (DIC). At the head of the deal was Dubai ruler Sheikh Mohammed bin Rashid al Maktoum, someone who could not just attempt to keep up with Abramovich but compete on a level playing field financially. Things didn't go to plan though and the company began to drag their heels over how much money they were paying each share. Rumours also swirled that they planned to sell the club again in seven years and like the Glazers would borrow heavily to finance the deal to buy the club. Moores who only wanted the best for Liverpool had second thoughts after these reports emerged and it was then that George Gillett's interest began. His initial hopes of buying Liverpool had been dashed by a lack of cash but the Montreal Canadiens ice hockey owner returned to the bargaining table with a business partner – Tom Hicks. To win the board over they offered £500 per share more, offering £5000 per share. This decision wasn't just Moores and was the whole board, and they decided to vote in favour of the Americans. The Americans paid £174m for the shares and promised to pay off £45m of club debt and put £215m towards the building of the new stadium. "I am handing this club on into safe hands," said Moores. Moores would walk away with £88m from the £174m deal, £8m more than what he would have made with DIC. "This is not someone coming over just to make a quick buck. I have made the right decision." Something that would unfortunately come back to haunt Moores and see his long relationship with the club and its fans be destroyed, based on his decision to sell to the Americans. Gillett and Hicks first press conference on February 6th 2007, provided all the sound bites fans wanted to here:

"We have purchased the club with no debt on the club" - George Gillett, lying from the minute he stepped through the door.

"This is not a takeover like the Glazer deal at Manchester United. There is no debt involved. We believe that as custodians of this wonderful, storied club we have a duty of care to the tradition and legacies of Liverpool."-
Tom Hicks, a leveraged buyout specialist, trying to buy on the cheap with leveraged money and selling high for a profit.

"We are going to build the finest team for the finest stadium in the Premier League and that is Liverpool" -
Tom Hicks, they hoped to build a stadium using the banks' money. But the world recession wrecked any hopes of borrowing more to build a new stadium and £30million per year went on paying interest on the debts

197

"The shovel needs to be in the ground in the next 60 days" -
George Gillett, just an idiotic comment to make, one that he
would never be able to achieve, just making a rod for his own
back.

"It's all about the fans and the winning tradition" –
George Gillett, it was never about the fans for them both, the club
was a business and an opportunity to make money, turning the
fans to declare arms on the owners, like never before in the
history of the club.

"Give us a little time, we're gonna have some fun together"-
George Gillett, if fun was a living nightmare for most fans, then
George was somewhat telling the truth.

"The more I looked the more I became convinced it was an
opportunity to buy a crown jewel of sports at a modest price"-
Tom Hicks, a slight truth from the whole interview, he realised it
was a business opportunity he couldn't turn down. Liverpool had
been underperforming commercially and with the club's global
fanbase they saw the chance to make a quick buck.

The following month and, "If Rafa said he wanted to buy Snoogy
Doogy we would back him". A personal favourite quote from
George Gillett, I think tongue in cheek, unless he'd been taking
scouting reports from Joe Kinnear. But there was some truth to
the team being improved and Liverpool manager Rafa Benitez
was able to sign Fernando Torres and Javier Mascherano. Torres
was a record transfer for Liverpool of £26.5m, who would go on
to become a fan favourite instantly, creating an unstoppable
partnership with Steven Gerrard.
A banner on the kop read at the time:
Match ticket….. £32

New anfield….. £220m
Rafa Benitez….. priceless
For everything else….. there's Tom and George

The team looked in a good position on the pitch to compete
again, even if the Snoop Dogg deal didn't come off unfortunately.
However, off the pitch things had already started to begin to
unravel. Moores may have got personal assurances that there
would be no debt loaded on the club but there was no legal
guarantee. Parry and Moores had also done their due diligence on
Gillett, but because Hicks came late to the table, they had virtually
no information on his past. "We had looked into Gillett's affairs
in detail, and he came up to scratch," Moores said. "To a great
extent we took Tom Hicks on trust, on George's say so." Just
months after their takeover though, the club was riddled with
debt, a promise already broken. Disunity and back-stabbing then
began, and the pair fell out quickly and with that more promises
were broken. "It soon became clear that they had very different
philosophies on how the club should be run," Parry said. "One
was hands off, the other hands on; one courted publicity, the
other didn't."

 Only a year after their takeover and Gillett wanted out already.
Hicks however had other plans and wouldn't allow Gillett to sell
as the power of veto due to his 50% share. At this time, they
rejected another approach from Sheikh Mansour, with Hicks
turning down a £500m deal, claiming it was 'derisory', something
he would come to regret come the end of their tenure. But the
cash had now completely dried up, with Benitez now being
ghosted as his calls across the Atlantic were ignored by the
owners. Like a husband and wife during a divorce, the pair would
air the club's dirty linen to the public, with probably the worst PR
stunt known to man. Hicks sat in his home in Dallas, with a live

broadcast through a Sky TV crew. Clutching his Liverpool mug, watching the side in action on a big screen with his kids around him in club merchandise, he demanded the resignation of chief executive Rick Parry. With Gillett refusing to agree to Hicks' request, Parry battled on before deciding to walk away in February 2009. "My position became untenable," he said. "The structure we had was dysfunctional and something had to give."

The fans were obviously worried about what was going on at the club, but when Hicks then decided to try to court Jurgen Klinsmann to become the new manager of Liverpool, behind Rafael Benitez's back, this would not stick with fans. "We attempted to negotiate an option as an insurance policy to have him (Klinsmann) become manager if Rafael left for Real Madrid or other clubs that were rumoured in the press", Hicks confirmed in a news conference in January 2008. Around this time saw the formation of the Spirit of Shankly (SOS), a fan group formed to represent the views of members and by extension all supporters of LFC. SOS' website reads, "We have proved, and continue to do so, that if we as supporters stand together and speak with one voice we can make a genuine difference to our football club, the city of Liverpool and the wider footballing world. Unity is strength."

The first official protest was organised on 22nd February 2008. It was planned after it was revealed that Tom Hicks Jr. would be attending the game that day. Members remained in the stadium, singing anti-owner songs, and displaying banners showing their displeasure towards the owners. Protests would continue for the next few years, with support building but also tensions between non-members and members, who believed it wasn't the 'Liverpool Way' to speak out against the owners of the club. The same day for a reason only Hicks Jr will know, he decided to go to the

Sandon pub to share a 'drink' with the fans. How he thought in his right mind this would go well, when literally fans were calling for the sale of the club they loved, due to the ownership of his Father and Business 'Partner'. It is inexplicable that he thought this would go well and turned into an ugly situation for Hicks Jr. Another attempt at a PR stunt that would drastically backfire. He started by taking pictures outside the pub before then entering with a team of bodyguards and ordering a drink from the bar. After people began to realise who he was after hearing his voice, people began to question what he was going to do with club and whether DIC would finally purchase the club. Thinks became tenser as more people arrived and people had an opportunity to air their anger towards one of the sons of their owners. Protest songs rained down on Hicks Jr and the anger was there for him and his minders plain to see. One of these songs aimed at the owners was "you lying B*****ds get out of our club," this was now being sung with 'club' replaced with 'pub', at which point he decided to abort the mission to get fans on side. As he tried to leave and his bodyguards formed a protective ring, Hicks Jr was swilled with a pint and another fan spitting in his direction. What had been an attempt to build some bridges, showed the owners failure to understand English fan culture and a clear failure for the owners to grasp how unpopular they have become.

Hicks Jr told the Liverpool ECHO after the incident, "I went to Sandon with some friends because I have wanted to go for quite some time to see the birthplace of the club. I also wanted the opportunity to have a direct talk with some of the supporters. I respect that some patrons have major disagreement with us, but that comes with the territory. I did have several constructive conversations in my short visit and look forward to following up with them next time I am in Liverpool.

Then came the introduction of someone who would complete the three musketeers, in managing director Christian Purslow, Royal Bank of Scotland played a key role in his appointment and his task was to raise £100m of investment to pay down the loans. It didn't take long for Benitez though to draw battles lines and he was at war with Purslow, complaining he was being undermined by Purslow and even angrier that the cost of new contracts for players was being taken out of his already depleted transfer kitty. To show the effect off field problems were now having on the pitch, in the space of 12 months Liverpool finished second in the league in May 2009, before then finishing seventh the season after and Benitez out the door. The season they finished second was an opportunity missed and with a better bench Liverpool should've won the league, at times having Nabil El-Zhar up front alone in draws that would ultimately cost them the league. A couple of late goals too from an Italian teenager, Federico Macheda securing United vital wins in the run in, and the league was lost, despite demolishing their rivals 4-1 at Old Trafford in the last few months of the season. Worse to was to come though, as the owners decided to appoint Roy Hodgson as Benitez's replacement, who had last won a title a decade earlier, with a Danish title.

The recruitment that summer, although he was on a shoestring and was horrendous, free signings of Joe Cole (unfortunately past it at this point with injuries), Christian Poulsen (maybe he was good when Hodgson worked in the Danish league) and Milan Jovanovic (made David N'Gog look like Thierry Henry in comparison) were the writing on the wall for how the season would go. Worse they spent money on bringing Paul Konchesky to come and play for Liverpool. It was my worst time as a Liverpool fan watching Liverpool as I travelled every week home and away across the country, witnessing a team that two seasons before had a midfield trio of Alonso, Maschaerano and Gerrard, now featured Poulsen, Meireles and Lucas, with Liverpool's two main players Gerrard and Torres out for large portions of the season. Wolves at home in December, and it was clear there was no coming back for Hodgson. Like with the protest's against the owners, that was uncharacteristic, for fans to turn on the manager, showed the depths the club had fallen too. Home fans sung for "Dalglish" and "Hodgson for England" due to rumours of Hodgson's link to the job, after the disastrous 2010 FIFA World Cup Campaign. Home fans even joined in with away supports chants of "You're getting sacked in the morning". That defeat at home was then followed by a loss to Blackburn away 3-1, a third defeat in four, leaving the club in 12th position, just four points clear of the relegation zone. Fans wishes were granted as Dalglish returned, after Hodgson left by mutual consent, bringing some rest bite to struggling fans.

Off the pitch, things had continued to deteriorate. Hicks Jr had a rush of blood to the head again and ended up having to resign as Liverpool director in January 2010. This time he made the sensible decision to being arguing via email with an SOS member, in which he called the fan an *idiot*, before responding with a further reply which said: *Blow me f**k face. Go to hell, I'm sick of you.* The full emails were never released but the damage was done. A spokesperson for SOS stated, "For one of the directors of the club, and the son of one of the owners, to respond to a fan with genuine concerns in such a manner is unacceptable. Tom Hicks Jr should resign, as his position as a director is now untenable.". The club released a statement confirming his resignation soon after. The Managing Director didn't learn from Hicks Jr, calling the supporters group 'Sons of Strikers'. In response a new flag appeared on the Kop, on a 15-foot flagpole. It is unconventional in shape, being a tall, thin rectangle, and on it is painted a giant penis with an angry red tip and the letters "P-U-R-S-L-O-W" daubed on the shaft. February 2010, then saw the launch of a billboard campaign across Merseyside with the message, "Tom & George: Not Welcome Here" and directions of how to join SOS. Finally, RBS' patience with the American reached its limit. April 2010x saw them reject an offer of £118m from the New York-based private equity firm Rhone Group for 40% of the club. RBS' response was to offer a final six-month extension of the loan, but with the stipulation that British Airways chairman Martin Broughton, was now appointed as an independent chairman to sell the club and crucially having the casting vote on the board.

A "Tom and George - Not Welcome Anywhere" Campaign was started on 29 June 2010 to show the depth of feeling from Spirit Of Shankly members and Liverpool supporters all around the world. Pictures came in from Anfield to Australia, Belfast to Bangkok. It was also reported by various media outlets around the world including Spanish newspaper Marc's and even in Tom Hicks' hometown of Dallas. SOS then declared independence from their American owners on 4th July 2010, American Independence Day, with a organised rally at St. George's Hall; attended by large numbers. There it was outlined how they aimed to try to allow the supporters to buy the club through a credit union partnership. The day saw them supported with speeches and backing from many prominent figures in the city, including: ex-Liverpool players John Aldridge and Howard Gayle; Comedians John Bishop and Neil Fitzmaurice; Members of Parliament Steve Rotheram and Alison McGovern; General Secretary of the Communication Workers Union Billy Hayes (trade unionist); Karen Gill, the granddaughter of Bill Shankly; and music by John Power, Pete Wylie, Ian McNabb, Peter Hooton, John O'Connell and Sons of Anfield. With Broughton in charge of finding a seller, interest was shown but nothing firm followed. The October 2010 deadline approached for the loan to be repaid to RBS, and even at this point Hicks was still trying to raise cash to clear the debt and remain in control. The future continued to look bleak and Liverpool FC the most successful football club in England, were on the brink of existing no more. Enter Liverpool's saviours New England Sports Ventures (more commonly known as FSG). The British courts declared that their bid of £300m could legally be accepted and they took over the club. Hicks and Gillett claimed Broughton had undervalued the club and called it an "epic swindle".

Their claims for compensation through British and American courts, were both thrown out. Their official statement read: "Attorneys say ludicrous, self-serving and illegal behaviour from directors and outsiders to hinder the club for years. It's an extraordinary swindle and it will result in exactly the wrong thing for the club and the fans" - statement from Tom Hicks and George Gillett as the club is handed over to Fenway Sports Group, Oct 2010. Even after they had lost their control of the club, they still spouted lies, showing how low they would stoop for the sake of money.

The new owners met the board of SOS on 18th October 2010, attempting to start right away with the process of repairing relations with the fans. At that meeting new Liverpool owner John Henry said to the members of the group present "You guys need to know that without the action and hard work of the Spirit of Shankly, Tom (Werner) and I would not have bought the Club". A slight twist in the tale and something I discovered in the research for this book is that FSG themselves received a loan from the same bank, RBS, with a £92m loan to help the complete the deal. Since then, obviously there has been no discussion around the further loans and with the club now in a better financial position, they haven't suffered the same fate as their predecessors and paid off the loan.

Football finance expert and life-long Liverpool fan Professor Rogan Taylor, director of The University of Liverpool's football industry group, told the Liverpool Echo in 2015, "It was a terrible period for the club. It was a disastrous delay in the club being able to reform itself and sort the stadium out and get itself in the kind of model that would work in the modern age. "He pointed to the large sums being spent by Chelsea which had edged Liverpool out of its traditional top four status in the Premier League. "There was no way Hicks and Gillett were going to make the investment that had to be done to give Liverpool a fighting chance."

The timing of their takeover in 2007 was bad. At the time money was still plentiful but the credit crunch and recession put an end to that. At the time of acquiring their loans/debts, it was at its most plentiful and at its cheapest. The fact they borrowed off RBS also didn't help them as it was one of the financial institutions worst hit by the financial crisis and was only saved by billions of pounds of British taxpayers' money. They relied too much on the risk of repaying loans and to do this it required CL qualification. In Benitez's last season finishing 7th may have been the final straw, as the lack of income from this and RBS not able to lend any more money, made it impossible for them to stay as owners. CL qualification was key for the club to sustain profitability and the position they found themselves in financially, made it paramount Liverpool qualified. Whether they were unlucky with the financial climate at the time, they lied from the beginning that loans wouldn't be used, so ultimately set themselves up to fail. Mr Justice Floyd who proceeded over the case said this, "They are guilty of unconscionable conduct, conclusively demonstrates just how incorrigible they are." Lots of people were caught in the crossfire of the mess these two fraudulent businessmen caused, no more so than David Moores. He unfortunately took the blame from some quarters for getting Liverpool into the mess, but his intention would never have been to see Liverpool find themselves in the position they were in. He had wanted what was best for the club and was unfortunately duped like many others were during their first press conference. The guilt of what happened forced him into a ten-year hiatus from Anfield before finally returning in 2019 for a 5-2 victory over Everton. Unfortunately, he passed away in 2022 at the age of 76. A tweet from Liverpool legend Kenny Dalglish best summed up his feelings and many others. "He was a loyal Liverpool fan whose dream came true when he was appointed Chairman, & he did a tremendous amount to help the Club. Our condolences go to his family. He'll be greatly missed by all who knew him. RIP."

John Aldridge former Liverpool striker said this about the club finally being sold. "I just felt so utterly elated. My first thought was "at least we're not going to become another Leeds United." That could have happened. We were losing £110,000 a day through interest on our debt. Once that was gone, we knew we had stability and therefore a chance. We could start again. In the end, hicks and Gillett were drowning men and they were pulling the club under with them. That afternoon it felt like we'd been given a life belt to get us to shore." The quote about "at least we're not going to become another Leeds United," is particularly reverberating as who knows where Liverpool would now be or if they'd even exist if the courts had ruled in favour of Hicks and Gillett. What happened to Leeds was down to foreign ownership though, but someone of the similar mould of Moores, a local businessman and fan. They were taken over in 1997/98 but a lifelong fan Peter Ridsdale. Like the Americans he promised Leeds fans the world. He promised to return the club to its former greatness, which is just what the fans wanted to hear, who felt they had been left behind by many of their domestic rivals. He would allow fans to live the dream, but it was short lived, and he would end up turning many fans dreams into a living nightmare in the space of six years. In 2000/2001 they reached the peak of the Ridsdale era, finishing in 3rd place and qualifying for the CL and reaching the UEFA cup semi-finals that season. Due to the increase in revenue generated by CL qualification, he took the same risk as the Glazers and Hicks and Gillett and gambled the club's future by taking out a £60m loan against future gate receipts to fund club spending. To be able to sustain these payments though they would need to consistently qualify for the CL. They had spent the money on addition players, which typically depreciate, which means CL qualification was imperative. A sign of the intent Ridsdale had was breaking the British transfer record to sign Rio Ferdinand for £18m from West Ham, in November 2000. The media at the time thought this showed how serious the club's ambition was, without highlighting the risky approach Ridsdale was taking.

The CL campaign would see them travel to the Bernabéu watching their side take Real Madrid to the wire in March 2001. They were finally knocked out by Valencia in the knockout stages. At that point no Leeds fan would foresee the position they would find themselves in three years later, relegated from the PL. Even worse a decade away from playing in the third tier of English football and on the brink of existence. The nightmare began by finishing fourth that season behind Liverpool by one point (at the time only 3 teams qualified for CL). Despite the failure to qualify Ridsdale continued throwing money around like it was going out of fashion. The season after they would fail to qualify again for the CL, this time finishing fifth. It now emerged that the club were approximately £80m in debt and needed to raise money by any means necessary. During the January transfer window of the 2002/3 season, they sold big name players: Robbie Keane, Olivier Dacourt, Jonathon Woodgate, Robbie Fowler and Rio Ferdinand. All were sold at alarmingly lower prices that they had been valued at, with only Ferdinand returning a profit at £30m to Manchester United. With a now depleted squad even the heroics of homegrown star Alan Smith, the club would be relegated in 2003/4. The Ridsdale dream was over and now a nightmare that would last longer than the dream had would begin. After three seasons in the Championship, Leeds hit rock bottom, with relegation to League One resulting in administration and the very existence of the club coming under threat. The club have now returned to the PL, returning in 2020, under the ownership of a foreign owner, Andrea Radrizzani, following a tumultuous period of ownership under another Italian Massimo Cellino, who although was controversial had returned the club to the Championship, before Radrizzani took over. Ridsdale had exposed a proud football institution to the dire perils that come when all-conquering greed meets unsustainable ambition. If this could happen to such a big club, then surely others were not immune from a debt-fueled crisis.

Others have not been so fortunate. Portsmouth won the FA cup in 2007/8, which allowed them to play in the UEFA cup the season after, defeating 7-time European champions AC Milan in the process. 2 years later in 2009/10 they would be taken over again this time by Saudi Arabian businessman Ali Al-Faraj. He was the third foreign owner the club had in 5 years, all had sold due to overspending or lack of finances to support the club going forward. Al-Faraj didn't pay the wages on time for 4 months that season. The club were relegated and were also issued with a winding up order for unpaid taxes. The club would find themselves relegated to League 2 by 2013, under more foreign ownership and financial issues, until the Pompey Supporters Trust became the new owners of the club on 10th April 2013. They have now returned to League one but have fallen short of returning to the Championship.

Other clubs have also been unable to pay off its existing debts. At this time the clubs have entered administration, in effect declaring bankruptcy. The clubs are then forced to be sold or stop operating completely. Crystal Palace, Wigan Athletic, Derby County, Bournemouth, Southampton, Leicester City and Bolton Wanderers, have all suffered similar fates. Cardiff forever known as the "Bluebirds' had their kit changed to red by Malaysian owner Vincent Tan, completely taking away the club's identity. The book has focussed on the effect football has had on people's mental health. Ownership of football clubs has had a direct effect on people and their mental health. People lose their livelihoods due to poor ownership, losing jobs due to the poor financial management of clubs, sometimes being unpaid for months, as they try to survive and keep their family afloat. This involves players and other club staff. The effect it has on fans can also be untold too, football is a release for lots and bad ownership has caused many untold stresses and for some, they have lost the club they love so much.

This has been the case with Bury, Rushden and Diamonds, Chester City, Macclesfield Town, Aldershot Town and Maidstone United. Fans have lost the club they loved and followed for their whole lives, as they now cease to exist in the form, they may have known their whole life. At a time, this looked a reality for myself as a lifelong fan of Liverpool, but how I would've coped if it had become a reality, doesn't bare to think about. For non-football fans it may be difficult to comprehend, but the club you support becomes your life and to have that taken away by dodgy businessman, who have no worries except for making themselves money. If a club does have the unfortunate fate some have faced and do enter administration, it costs these people nothing, everything they have paid for is through loans and therefore they can leave a club in these positions with no concern for their own welfare or their families futures, leaving local people and those involved in clubs, in crisis, mentally and financially.

8
Governance

**"FIFA cannot sit by and see greed rule the football world.
Nor shall we."**

Sepp Blatter, Former FIFA President in 2005

Sepp Blatter in 2005, condemned Europe's elite clubs, saying they
were threatening the future of the game. He didn't hold back in
his interview with the Financial Times, describing the transfers in
the modern market as.
"social and economic rape".
His attack was focussed mainly on the wealthy owners of the PL,
calling them businessmen who use football as a vehicle for profits
and profile. His interview produced lots of sound bites but what
he describes in the interview is very true, the issue is it's coming
from someone who isn't truthful at all. I will use snippets from
the interview throughout the chapter as we focus on greed and
governance's role in this.

The previous chapter focussed on ownership in the PL and in
some ways, Blatter alluded correctly even back in 2005 how
football was going.
*"A fortunate few clubs are richer than ever before. What
makes this a matter of concern is that, all too often, the source
of this wealth is individuals with little or no history of
interest in the game, who have happened upon football as a
means of serving some hidden agenda,"* said Blatter.

To combat this, he set up a task force to focus on corruption and ownership issues in the game. Like I've already pointed out, greed is one of the main driving forces behind football and Blatter knows that too.

"If we're not careful, football may degenerate into a game of greed - a trend I will vigorously oppose. This cannot be the future of our game. FIFA cannot sit by and see greed rule the football world. Nor shall we."

This is an interesting point as Blatter doesn't want greed to rule football, yet he is part of an organisation who has put their own greedy needs above that of the footballing world they're meant to serve.

Lots of this greed and corruption from FIFA and Blatter's role in this has been shown in Netflix's "FIFA Uncovered" documentary series. However, this was not the first time this had been brought to light. Most sensible football fans had already suspected that not everything was above board with the world football's governing body. A British reporter named Andrew Jenkins caused much shock and controversy when he released a book in May 2006 called, "Foul! The Secret World of FIFA: Bribes, Vote-Rigging and Ticket Scandals". Some 16 years profit to Netflix's documentary he also produced an episode for BBC panorama. In the documentary, the former chairman of the English Football Association, Lord Triesman, described FIFA as 'behav[ing] like a mafia family'. Blatter said in the 2005 interview that "FIFA cannot sit by and see greed rule the football world." However, the cash-for-contracts scandal shows precisely that greed ruled FIFA and many of their decisions. FIFA had a previous marketing partner called International Sport and Leisure (ISL). ISL were accused of paying large bribes to senior officials at FIFA, namely, Nicolas Leoz, Issa Hayatou and Ricardo Teixeira, from 1989 until 1999.

The bribes, according to ISL insiders, were necessary to ensure that the company was awarded the marketing contract for numerous World Cups. This came to light after ISL collapsed in 2001, due to debts of around £153m. This led to a free for all for various marketing companies as they seemed to arrange the sale of the TV coverage for the World Cup. It is alleged that this TV rights rigging dates to 1991. To outline how FIFA member's made money off this, you can look at the TV rights for the 2010 and 2014 World Cups. The rights were bought for $600,000 to a TV company owned by a FIFA member Jack Warner. The company he bought them with then sold them on to a different company for $18 million, earning a profit of £17.4 million. This is on top of the fact that they also receive bribes from the companies who end up purchasing the rights. This shows an example of the huge amount of money they were able to make for themselves. This money is what has tempted so many of the officials to eat the forbidden fruit.

Blatter in his role as President of FIFA, has seen the organisation be dogged with allegations of corruption since he took over in 1998 from João Havelange. Havelange was a White Brazilian business with links to his own country's military government. He tried to present himself as a radical alternative, that would champion poorer football-playing countries. David Conn in his brilliant book "The Fall of the House of FIFA" said this about Havelange. "Havelange did, without question, help himself to bribes," Conn writes. The Brazilian played a central part in "instituting a culture of corruption" at FIFA – a culture of favours strategically handed out and reliably reciprocated, which helped keep him in office for almost a quarter of a century, from 1974 to 1998. It can be said that modern football dates to him starting as FIFA president in 1974. Before this FIFA had just been a small outfit, who were a group of men who would simply organise the

World Cup tournament. João Havelange changed this. He promised the global expansion of the game, but due to the previous regime funds were not available for this. To create these funds, he began to seek sponsorship deals. Football just as sport for its own sake? That option no longer existed. Now it was brought to you in association with Coca-Cola and Adidas.

The first sign of what was to come in terms of how host nations would be chosen despite political issues surrounding that nation started in 1978. When Havelange endorsed the 1978 World Cup, hosted by Argentina despite the country having recently fallen to a vicious military dictatorship. What he also saw was an opportunity to expand and exploit the sport's marketing and broadcast potential. The previously mentioned ISL was setup by Adidas owner Horst Dassler. All of FIFA's rights were outsourced to this company. Huge money started to be made, but instead of member nations seeing their fair share or FIFA itself. Havelange made sure he himself was lavishly rewarded. He did this throughout his tenure, and this would be used against him by his understudy Blatter to finally take control in 1998. Despite this though, Havelange remained honorary FIFA president until 2013, when his bribe-taking was finally officially exposed. He was 96 years old. Even after Blatter took over thought it is suggested that people continued to further their own interests through bribes, cash-for-votes and even money laundering. What makes Blatter even more suspicious in his role enabling this is that he was responsible for the abandonment of numerous investigations into the dodgy realising of the organisation he run.

"I find it unhealthy, if not despicable, for rich clubs to send scouts shopping in Africa, South America and Asia to 'buy' the most promising players there. Dignity and integrity tend to fall by the wayside in what has become a glorified body

215

market. Europe's leading clubs conduct themselves increasingly as neo-colonialists who don't give a damn about heritage and culture but engage in social and economic rape by robbing the developing world of its best players."

To draw comparison between Europe's top teams' treatment of young talent and slavery may seem a bit extreme, but there is reason behind his extremism. In terms of the statistics around his comments, there is clear evidence that European clubs have used Africa and South America to find players. Football Benchmark, who study player trends around the globe looked at the number of African players plying their trade in Europe. They looked at the 11 prominent top tier leagues in Europe and the number of African nationals playing in these top tiers. It is important to note that the primary nationality was the key criteria; players of African origin who play for non-African national adult teams were excluded from the analysis. The report found that more than 500 African footballers are contracted by these clubs' first teams in the 11 leagues, which constitutes approximately 6% of their total player base. Unsurprisingly, most of them come from West-African countries. South American footballers have also been an integral part of football in Europe for decades.

The globalisation of the transfer market in the 90s saw their numbers explode, to the point where now there are practically no leagues in the UEFA region without a South American player. What Blatter points to though and is also the case with African players is that there is a huge financial disparity between European clubs and the rest of the world. This creates a "talent drain" system, through which many players move to Europe at a very young age and spend their prime career years there. The best South American players will be found in one of the "Big Five" leagues. As of July 2022, there were 218 players from South

America (CONMEBOL) at European "Big Five" league clubs. Not counting European nationalities, only Africa (CAF) had more players than that (246 in total). LaLiga has the most (70), which is not a surprise as many South American players prefer this as their destination due to the language and the cultural similarities with their home countries. The PL is in second place just ahead of Serie A. What makes the PL standout ahead of the rest though is the total estimated value of the South American players in their league. It is by far the highest in the PL, which indicates that many highly rated South American stars end up playing there during their peak years. Eight different Premier League sides currently have at least one CONMEBOL nationality player who is valued at EUR 30+ million.

However, like with everything else Blatter says, we cannot believe the only purpose for these comments were to highlight the injustices he felt European clubs showed through 'glorified body market'. Although there has been a huge growth in the number of Asian players in European leagues, it is a number that is significantly below that of African and South American players. Especially in 2005 when this number was significantly lower again. It is the inclusion of this continent which really outlines the real reason for Blatter's comments. After originally taking over in 1998, Blatter won four more elections during his presidency. Throughout this time, he managed to avoid being uncovered as a corrupt official for years. The most likely reason for this was due to his determination to increase the influence of countries in Africa and Asia, thereby winning himself support. As FIFA is currently set up, each country that is part of the organisation gets an equal vote on FIFA related matters. As such, the African and Asian countries that have never won a major tournament have as much say in matters as Germany, the country that has appeared in eighteen World Cups and won four of them. Some of the exposes from the reports into the corruption highlight how bribes were used both ways between FIFA and these associations. There was "$1,983 spent by the AFC [Asian Football Confederation] ... on 14 shirts" for Blatter. A whistle-blower from the tiny Bahamas football association bravely exposing a bribery operation via a "brown envelope of cash down his trousers"; and a "centre of excellence" for football in Trinidad, built with "at least $25.95m" of FIFA money, including "conference and banquet halls ... a hotel ... a swimming-pool complex" and pitches where a visitor says they, "did not find much football going on".

These smaller nations had the same voting rights as major football hubs and would then be allowed to have a say in who became president or where the World Cup would be held. Men such as Jack Warner, the president of Concacaf (the Confederation of North, Central America and Caribbean Association Football), and his sidekick, the American sports administrator Chuck Blazer, took full advantage. We mentioned earlier how Warner had benefited from the sales of TV rights through his own companies, but he also been found to have been involved in lots more greed and corruption. In 2006, a FIFA inquiry by consultants Ernst and Young, found that his son Daryan had picked up tickets for the 2006 World Cup. These FIFA tickets were then provided to a travel company called Simpaul, which was owned by the family and were then sold at a premium value above face. For this he was reprimanded by FIFA and Blatter, but no action was taken, as they said it couldn't be proven that he knew about it. Another incident came in 1989, when his nation Trinidad were playing the USA to qualify for the 1990 World Cup. The game required the home nation to draw to qualify for their first World Cup. Taking advantage of this Warner, oversold tickets for the game. There were terrible overcrowding and said that he had sold 15,000 more tickets. However, despite this being known a judicial inquiry never reported.

In FIFA Uncovered, one of the main topics discussed with Blatter, is how much guilt he feels for the fact he presided over an executive committee that was overwhelmingly bent that only one of the twenty-two members in the committee, when Russia and Qatar were awarded the 2018 and 2022 World Cups, is still actually in the post. He did express regret for this but denies any moral responsibility. He instead turns on those who ensured he stayed in place, saying he can't be expected to answer for other committee members from "other countries and other cultures". This is particularly interesting as the worst scandals involved delegates from African, Middle Eastern and Caribbean nations. Some of those who he wanted to protect from European 'predators.'

Since the vote, 16 of 22 voting exco members present in that hall have been implicated in or investigated over some form of alleged corruption or bad practice. This all resulted in the most significant scandal in footballing history, some would argue the biggest in all sport alongside the truth about Lance Armstrong. In 2015 saw the arrests and subsequent investigations of many members of the FIFA committee, with the FBI producing a 47-count indictment against assorted footballing figures. Julio Grondona, 26 years a Fifa executive, died in 2014 and has been safely loaded with blame by his old pals. Jack Warner, 79 years old and still going about his business in Trinidad, remains the key suspect for the US Department of Justice.

Ultimately the chief players behind this double World Cup bid spectacular were Blatter, Michel Platini (UEFA President), Vitali Mutko (Russia's bid supremo), Mohammed bin Hammam (the

Qatari president of the Asian Football Confederation), Nicolas Sarkozy (the president of France), and Putin. Throughout it all though, none of the accusations have touched Qatar themselves, who remain blameless and a spectator to the arraignment of others. The accusations levelled against the chief players are shocking.

The downfall of Sepp Blatter and the disgraced FIFA president's one-time heir apparent, Michel Platini, came about after they were banned from football for eight years by the world governing body's own ethics committee. Both men were cleared of corruption charges but found guilty of a series of other breaches including a conflict of interest and dereliction of duty over a 2m Swiss francs (£1.35m) "disloyal payment" from Blatter to Platini, the UEFA president, in 2011. Neither man was able to provide a written contract for the £1.35m payment or definitively explain why it was eventually paid in 2011, a few weeks before a presidential election at a time when Blatter was facing a challenge from Mohamed bin Hammam. Platini acted as a special adviser to Blatter from 1998 to 2002. The Frenchman claimed Blatter told him at the time that FIFA could not afford to pay him, despite the governing body making £78m over that four-year cycle and did not want to break its wage structure. Blatter and Platini said they believed their verbal contract were legal under Swiss law. However, Swiss law places a five-year time limit on such payments. In addition to alleged corruption, which carried a potential lifetime ban, the charges were based on four other potential breaches: mismanagement, conflict of interest, false accounting, and non-cooperation with the ethics committee. The judges said: "Neither in his written statement nor in his personal hearing was Mr Blatter able to demonstrate another legal basis for this payment. By failing to place FIFA's interests first and abstain from doing anything which could be contrary to FIFA's interests,

Mr Blatter violated his fiduciary duty to FIFA. His assertion of an oral agreement was determined as not convincing and was rejected by the chamber." Platini, the ethics committee judges said, also placed himself in a position of a conflict of interest and violated his fiduciary duty to FIFA. "Mr Platini failed to act with complete credibility and integrity, showing unawareness of the importance of his duties and concomitant obligations and responsibilities." Blatter acknowledged an administrative error in failing to register FIFA's debt to Platini in its accounts for eight years, though he insisted: "This is nothing to do with the ethics regulations."

In 2011 the Sunday Times printed a story alleging that Bin Hammam had made payments to football power brokers totalling $5m via 10 slush funds. Bin Hammam, it was said, hosted backslapping junkets where cash was handed out. He allegedly paid $1.6m into a bank account controlled by Warner, half of it before the vote for the World Cup. He allegedly paid the Somali Football Federation $100,000 through his daughter's bank account. With no supposed reason at all. Bin Hammam has been banned for life from football, then unbanned, then re-banned. He's seen as a hero in Doha. He's 73 years old and will take his role to the grave, with no threat of further repercussions.

In 2019 there were allegations FIFA had benefited from a $400m rights deal with Al Jazeera, Qatar's state TV station, offered just 21 days before the bid decision, with an extra $100m top-up should Qatar succeed. FIFA denies this was material to any decision made.

The Garcia report revealed that Sandro Rosell an exco member, had connected dealings with Qatar, made a payment of €1.45m to the bank account of Qatari clients then 10-year-old daughter. Rosell had previously sent an email to his Qatari contact promising: "This means I'll be able to invest this money for my interest, that I hope, finally, will be yours." There was also mention of lucrative friendly fixtures, of Qatari gas deals, of projects funded, by Michel D'Hooghe, Belgian exco member, being "compromised" by the offer of a job for his son at Qatar's Aspire Academy.

Plus, there is the other major set piece of that bid period, the lunch at the Élysée Palace in November 2010 when Sarkozy, France's president, hosted Platini and the emir of Qatar. Platini switched his vote to Qatar around this time. He denies the two events were connected. The emir's government would later buy out Paris Saint-Germain, increase its stake in a French media group and buy up the rights to French football. France has enjoyed productive commercial relations with Qatar ever since. Everybody present denies there is any connection.

Blatter, Platini and Bin Hamman remain banned from football, however Blatter and Platini have been cleared of corruption charges in July 2022. Sarkozy has a criminal conviction for dubious election practice. Mutko has been implicated in a state-sponsored doping scandal. Whilst Putin is arguably one of the most hated people in the world now and is waging a land war in Europe.

"Having set foot in the sport seemingly out of nowhere, they proceed to throw pornographic amounts of money at it."

Abramovich like we pointed out changed the whole scope of football transfers. There was finally someone to compete with the money spent by the 'Galacticos'. The previous chapter showed some of the ludicrous amounts that have been spent by clubs in

Europe's top 5 leagues, clearly showing that the PL is out in front of spending, like was highlighted by Blatter even back in 2005. In 2023 the gross transfer spends across the 'big five' leagues totalled €4.5bn in this summer's window, a €1.6bn (52%) increase on the previous year (summer 2021: €3.0bn). Despite this growth, spending among Europe's top leagues has not quite returned to pre-COVID levels (2017-19 three-year average: €4.7bn). Der Spiegel published 'football leaks' in 2016 up to 2018, which like 'wikileaks' did to governments around the world, shone football and its transfers in a shocking new light. The man in charge of tracking and reporting on these transfers for FIFA was Mark Goddard, who did this job until June 2017. He was the general manager of the FIFA subsidiary transfer matching system, which was tasked with enforcing transparency in transfers, admitted after football leaks that actual transfer fees could be twice as high as the FIFA figures. One of Football leaks aim was to make transfers more transparent and reduce the influence of player agents and investment funds that had a growing hold on football. UEFA's answer was to introduce 'Financial Fair Play (FFP)', in 2011, to stop clubs spending more than they earnt, but many found ways round this, whilst UEFA, have lacked strength in stopping clubs finding these adverse methods. Football Leaks once again has allowed us to see how clubs have done this.

The CIES Football Observatory added up the transfer fees paid by Manchester City over the last 10 years and arrived at a total of over £1.5bn. The team's financial resources seem unlimited. After all, it is owned by Sheikh Mansour bin Zayed Al Nahyan, a member of the Abu Dhabi ruling family.

A comprehensive file with documents from the Football Leaks database provides evidence of a system that was apparently used for several years:

- In 2012, a portion of the sponsorship money coming from Abu Dhabi was booked internally as "owner investment" – a sum of £150m
- In 2013, emails showed payment obligations being divided up according to "club direct payments" and "partner supplements." Within these emails it showed Etihad only had to pay £8m of the total sponsoring sum of £67.5m. According to the mail, the remaining £59.5m was extra – presumably paid by Sheikh Mansour.
- For the 2013-2014 season alone, the supplements from Abu Dhabi added up to £92.5m. The information pertaining to these supplements was not meant to be shared with outsiders: "We mustn't show the partner supplement if it is going outside the club," warned Andrew Widdowson, who was head of finance at the time, in early 2013.
- In September 2015 as well, club representatives differentiated between a payment of £60.25m and the £8m that Etihad "should be funding directly." Emails that were exchanged at the time about the share of sponsorship money that was to come "direct" from the company. The rest was apparently to come out of the budget of shareholder ADUG – Sheikh Mansour.
- In March 2016, the £8m payment relating to Etihad's sponsorship made yet another appearance.

Whereas the last two years of pandemic-related financial difficulties created significant problems for professional football teams across England and Europe, Manchester City managed to increase its marketing revenues in the first COVID affected season. At the beginning of the year, Manchester City were also able to add three new sponsors to its portfolio, all of which were headquartered in UAE.

According to Football Leaks, now FIFA President Infantino ensured that Manchester City and Paris Saint-Germain, both owned by emirates in the Gulf, received only mild penalties for their massive violations of UEFA's Financial Fair Play (FFP) rules. The rules stated that clubs' debts in the two seasons between 2011 and 2013 could only add up to a total of €45m. UEFA investigators and independent auditors found, however, that PSG's deficit was €218m and Man City's was €188m. As a result of those violations, the two clubs potentially faced being banned from participation in the Champions League, the harshest penalty. The Qatari owners of PSG and the owners of Manchester City, who come from Abu Dhabi, tried to prevent such a penalty by exerting massive pressure on UEFA leadership. Infantino at the time was the general secretary of the investigating commission. During this investigation process he held secret meetings with club leaders from Paris and Manchester on multiple occasions, provided them with confidential details and proposed compromises that he was not authorized to offer.

Through leaked emails it also shone a light on how he sketched out a suggested settlement with the association. "You will see that I've sometimes chosen a wording which 'looks' more 'strong,'" Infantino wrote, making it clear that he was willing to massage certain passages. "Please read the document with this spirit." Of course, Infantino continued, the document was just between the two of them, which is to say, highly confidential. In May 2014, the two clubs signed agreements with UEFA that hardly affected their bottom at all. A few days prior, Scottish economic expert Brian Quinn, who, as head of the FFP Investigatory Chamber, would have overseen the proceedings against the two clubs independent of UEFA leadership, resigned from his post. He believed the settlements were too lenient given the magnitude of the violations.

In the years following the settlements, PSG and Manchester City together spent more than a billion euros on new Players.

This year Manchester City have announced the highest commercial revenues in the history of English football, and publicly confirmed they remain under investigation by the Premier League over alleged financial irregularities. The Mail on Sunday uncovered new anomalies in one of City's most recent commercial partnerships. The deal in questions was with gambling firm 8xBet in the summer as they introduced 'a new regional partnership that will see the brand become the Official Betting Partner of the club in Asia.'

A glossy promotional video announced Teddy Sheringham as an 8xBet 'ambassador' The video depicts a woman apparently representing 8xBet shaking hands on that contract. The woman is a London-based model called Jasmine who more typically poses for bikini, lingerie and fashion shoots, and holds no role at 8xBet. The source says it is the 'regular practice' to use actors and models for such shoots.

A LinkedIn profile of someone claiming to be 8XBet's co-founder and CEO, Trinh Thu Trang, was deleted after it was shown her profile photo was a stock image. During their investigation, the Mail on Sunday established the same image was widely used across the internet, including on a sex site where the user was offering services as a bisexual 'cam model'.

An email address that was provided by City for the mail, for a man called Jet Zhu, the CEO of a Dubai-based marketing firm, QOO Global, and the de facto spokesman for 8xBet, to answer all questions related to the firm. Mr Zhu did not want to speak on the record, but a source said the Trinh Thu Trang profile was 'false' and not posted by anyone from 8xBet.

Zhu's own firm, QOO also had some peculiarities. The firms claim it has up to 50 employees, but their website only carries examples of work for one client: 8xBet. A source close to QOO said the marketing company was not able to name any other clients 'due to confidentiality'. Of QOO's employees, 23 apparently have LinkedIn profiles but these include a man based in Lahore, Pakistan who has a Facebook page promoting his work as a motivational speaker, and inspirational quotes by Martin Luther King. The man in question when contacted said he was the CEO of his own company, then claimed he was the CEO of QOO, which is not true. Asked if we could meet him at QOO's office in Dubai, he could not provide an address and said: 'We are working digitally from Pakistan and Dubai.'

Another supposed full-time Dubai-based QOO employee appears to work for a healthcare company while a third stopped answering questions when asked about 8xBet. A fourth has her own business offering website development and digital marketing services.

A source close to QOO said that personal social media profiles were not monitored by QOO and some people claiming false associations with QOO have been reported to LinkedIn. Requests for a company HQ address for 8xBet and a phone number were ignored. This whole investigation came a week after the Mail on Sunday reported that Fulham had dumped a commercial partner, Titan, following an investigation by the newspaper, showing it was 'staffed' by fake employees played by actors, and guaranteeing unrealistic financial returns of 'at least' 480 per cent profits per year.

Manchester City's annual accounts for 2021-22, published last week, showed their commercial revenues are now £309.5m, up 13% in a year and now more than half their total income. Commercial giants and cross-city rivals Manchester United earned only £258m from such deals in the same season. In their accounts, City also acknowledged 'an ongoing Premier League investigation' into alleged irregularities. These include alleged anomalous 'disguised investment' via sponsors, alleged violations of rules on signing underage players and alleged fictitious consultancy contracts. The investigation is well into a fourth year and moving especially slower as City's lawyers continue to contest its legitimacy. The one above example of the betting firm really does bring into question the legitimacy of other such deals.

Qatari Emir Tamim bin Hamad al Thani is using football for sport washing. They purchased PSG in 2011. QIA, invests profits from oil and gas and have interests in companies worth £338.4b. Before Neymar they had spent £700m on players. That has now risen by another £500m with the signing of Neymar and Mbappe for around £200m with bonuses too. This along with the World Cup is their way of improving their global image, winning the CL is their aim with PSG. The original deal for Mbappe showed how easy it was for them to get round FFP by Monaco sending him on a free loan, before then £90m being sent to them in the first year and £55m in the second year.

PSG, who reportedly made a total loss of €574million between 2020 and 2022, were still able to lure superstar Kylian Mbappe away from Real Madrid in 2022, with a lucrative £650,000-a-week contract. LaLiga league President Javier Tebas, published a formal letter to UEFA outlining LaLiga's disapproval of the contract extension, has told L'Equipe via Mundo Deportivo that PSG deserved 'immediate sanctions'. He said: '10 million euros for PSG and its president (Nasser Al-Khelaifi) is like a cup of coffee.' The 60-year-old went on to accuse the Ligue 1 club of 'breaking the ecosystem of football.'

PSG signed former Barcelona star Neymar Jr for a world record fee of £198m from the LaLiga giants in 2017 and have since assembled one of the most lucrative teams on the planet, with superstars such as Lionel Messi, Marco Verratti and Gianluigi Donnarumma. Despite Tebas' protestation, LaLiga giants Barcelona, Real Madrid and Atletico Madrid have each amassed sporting debts of around €1billion (£867m) or more. Barcelona, who utilised various economic levers this summer to sign and register new summer signings including Robert Lewandowski, Raphinha and Jules Kounde. They reportedly still owe Manchester City £46m for the transfer of Ferran Torres in January 2022.

Third party ownership first came to light when there was a link between FC Twente and a company called doyen sports in 2014. The investment model would be banned 15 months later by FIFA. The third-party ownership (TPO) is a gamble on humans, more so footballers. They buy shares in a football transfer rights. A little like the doomed football index that bets on how well they perform and how their market value will rise. Once the player is sold the TPO then gets paid.

It's also used to ensnare clubs that are highly in debt. Twente win the league in 2010 but I'm doing so had overextended itself backed by wealthy fan Joop Munsterman. To be able to pay the wages they had used to secure the players to win the league. They would need to qualify for the cl each year. After the league win, they didn't manage this again, and were succumbed with debt by 2014. Instead of selling its expensive players and rebuilding with youth. They joined forces with a shady investor, introducing doyen sports.

Doyen is a sports rights company with HQ in Malta and London. They acquired shares in 5 players at the start of their careers for 5milliom euros. This was a win-win as Twente were well known for their excellent academy. The fine print made it impossible for them to lose money. What was worse is the club signed a deal that meant if they didn't sell a player against doyens wishes they would have to pay the investor. Basically, leaving them in charge of the make-up of the squad. To pay them off and get them out of their club they were forced to sell their best players. It brings into question the treatment of the fans who want to see the best players at their club, when really that player who shows promise must be sold at the first opportunity to pay off these investors. The deal was leaked by football leaks which caused fan protests and the dissolving of the deal, but not until doyen were paid 3.3 mil. The KNVB then revoked their first division licence but on appeal would be banned from Europe for 3 years instead. The one way they could try to get themselves out of the financial mess they had found themselves in.

Something some people don't know is that Atletico Madrid have funded most of their recent success through third party deals. An example of this was Saul Niquez, who had 40% of his transfer rights sold at 16 to a group of Irish investors for £1.5m. Over the last 8 years, they have won La Liga, the Europa League and reached two CL finals. The summer of 2015, saw them burdened with a £520m debt and £45m owed to Spanish tax authorities. Mostly due to the rule of former president Jesus Gil y Gil, who won once came to the stadium with a crocodile on a leash. When winning the league in 1996 he rode through the street atop an elephant. He died in 2004 and the club was in financial disaster.

His son Miguel Angel took over and is the main shareholder with 55%. They make profits from buying low and selling high. Some of their most recent high price sales included: Aguero- £36m to City, Falcoa- £43m to Monaco and Jackson Martinez- £42m Guangzhou. Investors from 2010 were allowed to buy shares in players transfer rights. It was them who decided to sell top players and fan favourites. Something Gil jr tried to keep a secret. The firm who had most of these were Doyen sports and Irish company Quality football- led by Peter Kenyon and Jorge Mendes. They advised who the investors should invest money in. The investors were guaranteed a minimum return of 10% annually. Atletico invested Mendes funds on the rights for 20 players at least for around £58m. This however meant they no longer had control over transfers and robbed the chance of fans identifying themselves with their favourites as they were sold as they as they became stars.

Aguero was bought with £2.5m of investments. A £2m investment bought 50% rights of Diego Costa, whilst £6m bought the same amount in Arda Turan. £5m bought the same 50% for Eduardo Salvio. All players were sold for considerably more than the initial amount invested, but this meant these amounts didn't all go back into the clubs' pockets, making the investors very rich in the process instead. Saul eventually failed but if his minimum release clause was met, he would've made £45m. Which would've been a profit of £16.5m for the investors. A return of more than 1000%. Escobar would've been proud of this return; the cocaine trade would struggle to make comparable returns. 5 days after an offer is received Quality Football is notified and then they decide whether they agree with the deal. Maybe explains the strange loan to Chelsea last year, which for the investors didn't pay off.

"What they do not understand is that football is more about grass-roots than idols; more about giving entertainment and hope to the many than bogus popularity to a predictable few."

The money that is in football is absurd and more of this needs to be pumped back into the grassroots. Many models around Europe work, but none of these countries are making the same amount of money as the PL. The FA's main role is to ensure that grass roots football thrives.

The FA website says we 'keep the grassroots game going'. The FA does a good job of running junior football around the country but lacks the resources to lead the way on protecting and growing grassroots football. The issue is the FA is reliant on others to fund the investment in facilities. In 2018, the FA invested £22.5m into the football foundation. Women's football has seen a huge boost, also helped by the publicity of the England's women's team. However, men's football continues to fall, and the quality of the facilities is a real issue. A Telegraph report in 2018 found some truly shocking statistics about the state of grassroots football in the country and in particular its facilities. It found that only one in three grassroots pitches are adequate. In the 2016/16 season there were 150,000 games called off due to poor facilities. One in six of these games that were called off were due to poor pitches. Most of the games called off were grass pitches, as 3G pitches can often overcome most conditions, except for the freezing conditions. But unbelievably, 33 out of the 50 county FAs in the country don't have their own 3G pitch. When you compare us to Germany, we have half the amount of 3G pitches that Germany have. The fact that these pitches could allow for football all year and deal with most weather conditions allowing more football to be played, keeping more people in the game. We have the richest league in the world, yet we are behind all our peers. The reason being no matter how hard the FA works their lack of influence over the PL finances is a major constraint on what they're able to do in its ability to deliver for the grassroots.

The mayor of Manchester Andy Burnham said this about how he saw things in relation to football and its grassroots, when he was Secretary of State for Culture, Media and Sport. "The grassroots are looking at a bleak decade if there is not change. It can't be difficult for football to create a per any revenue stream for the grass roots from agents and transfer fees, as well as betting and the tv deals- that could create a solid sustainable fund. The elite game depends directly on the grass roots- that's where the future revenue comes from." Burnham setup a football task force that managed to secure a 5% levy from the PL total income that would be given to good causes and the grassroots. But didn't believe the PL were committed to this. "I think the pl has always seen the 5% as slightly moveable recognisable commitment, we never saw it that way. We saw it as a clear commitment."

If the PL did stick to their commitment that this 5%, then this would amount to £165m from the £3.3b they earn. But if you look more closely into this money and how it is spent, the term 'good causes' doesn't just mean grassroots. If you breakdown how this money is spent, only a fraction is spent on grassroots. £110m is spent on wider football support, which is the payments to support the wider professional game, so the payments to teams outside the PL. The Pl always stress that from this money, so 90% of the money will go to the Football league and the two tiers below (Conference and Conference North/South). £6.5m is also spent on stadium improvements in these leagues. This is an important source of money to maintain the professional game and is why the English professional game does thrive in some ways, but this amount of money is going to Professional football not grassroots, does this really count towards what people think is 'good causes'. £13.4m is then given to wider football support for the development. £10.98m then goes to solidarity programmes, youth, and community development. So only a portion of this is going to grassroots. It should also be noted that they give £77m to charitable activities. £17.3m to the football foundation, who will spend money on grassroots and are a section of the FA. £25m goes to PFA charitable activities, to support former professionals in different ways. £34.5m is then sent to clubs to use to support their community activities and PL community activities.

When you factor in the amount spent on transfers it becomes even more clearer, how little actually goes back to grassroots football. To make it even worse you then look at the agent fees from the £1.9b spent on transfers. In 2018/19 the agent fees that year was £261m. None of which again will go back into the grassroots. Teams who don't remain in the PL also then receive £273m in parachute payments. All these are much higher amounts than the whole £165m given to 'good causes' and massively trump the actual amount that goes back into grassroots.

Lord Faulkner who was part of Burnham's task force, was one of the first to propose the 5% levy and offered a further solution. "The game has become fabulously wealthy, and I support the principle of an independent football commission which receives income from various sources and spends it on the interests of the game rather than be dependent on just the goodwill of the PL. A proportion would come from tv income. What would be quite good is if each transfer deal a proportion of the proceeds would go to the commission. It would not need to be a large proportion but would certainly mount up if it applied to everybody."

Mark Gregory, who works for Ernst and Youngs as Chief economist in the UK, wrote a brilliant book called "More than a game", which took an in depth look at the state of the finances in the PL. He also suggested a way that the money in the PL could be used to support the grassroots, also through and independent football commission. If the commission placed a 5% levy on transfers, this would generate £50m annually. If we then placed a 1% levy on wages, from the wage bill in the PL that is £3b+, could generate a further £30m. These two small things could generate a minimum of £80m a year alone for the grassroots, that could then be spent improving the state of the game. This is without even focusing on agent fees and other expenditures and incomes in the game.

The money that is spent by the PL on transfers and agents as well can be broken down more to see how it could influence the lower leagues, rather than using the 'good causes' levy to support them. From the £1.86b that was spent by PL clubs in 2018/19- 67% of this was spent on players outside of England. This is seven times the £175m that was spent on players in the football league. When you then also factor in the money that was also spent on players from other PL clubs, that accounted for £369m. This means that of the total amount spent of the £1.86b, only 19% reminded in England. When you look at when the PL started in 1992, only £75m was spent. Of this £46.5m (62%) remained in the top division, whilst the rest flowed from the clubs in the top division to the rest of British football, around a third of the money to lower league clubs. This meant hardly any of the money left England. Even worse is when you look at the money that was spent on agent fees to facilitate these transfers. In 2018/19 the fees amounted to £261m from PL clubs. In the football league this was £57m, mostly championship clubs. This means that there was more money paid to agents than the annual turnover of all the clubs in League 1 and League 2. Agent fees also accounted for 50% more than the transfer fees paid by PL clubs to Football League clubs, meaning clubs have spent more on an agent than actual homegrown players for their team. All this money could be levied and included in money that could then be spent on facilities and community activities, yet it is not.

The FA has no control over the finances of the PL as they're a separate entity and this is a major stumbling block for the FA and the money available to them. The FA therefore relies on the '5%' from the PL and other handouts from the government and schemes/charities. In real terms the FA is struggling for the money to sustain grassroots football to the level it needs to do, even just to try and match its other European counterparts let alone standout as the best around. A sign of the struggle was the fact the FA was willing to sell Wembley, the home of the England football team to Fulham and Jacksonville Jaguars (NFL) owner Shahid Khan. This proposed sale was set to take place in 2018, until unexpectedly Khan pulled out of the deal later the same year.

The then FA chairman, Greg Clarke and chief executive Martin Glenn had consistently argued for the sale, to release the £600m and further matched funding to improve grassroots, public football facilities throughout England which were and still are run-down and suffering from local authority budget cuts. This hasn't been renewed since, but this isn't due to the fact more money has been released to allow them to improve this. During the 2019 General Election, then Prime Minister Boris Johnson promised £550m towards grassroots sport in the country. This included building 2000 new 3G 11-a-side pitches and repairing 20,000 grass pitches across the country. He promised that within ten years, every family in the country would be a maximum of 15 minutes

236

away from a 'great' pitch. Furthermore, 40% of the spending would be spent in the most deprived areas in the country. Since them promises the pandemic hit and he's been busy with other promises he couldn't keep and not much has been seen of this promised vital funding. Operation 'Big picture' led by Liverpool and Manchester United which was unanimously rejected by the PL and the government, which would've seen many reforms of the PL, with also 25% of future TV deals being given to the Football league, along with £180m to grassroots football. Although, in essence it was rejected as 14 clubs had no say in the deal before it was released in the press, it looked to change the whole governance of the PL, for the best? Who knows? But it did set out to give more to grassroots that was for sure, if promises were kept.

"More about giving entertainment and hope to the many than bogus popularity to a predictable few."

Blatter talks about European football needing to be more about entertainment and hope, than what he describes as a 'bogus popularity'. When he talks about a 'predictable few', research shows that the competitive evolution of European football has started to reduce. Two Norwegian academics Haugen and Heen published a research paper: the competitive evolution of European top football- signs of danger. They focused on the balance of uncertainty of outcome, they measured it by comparing actual results with the predicted results. When looking at this is shows that since 1993, the 'big 5' leagues have all reduced. The reason they surmise in the paper is that due to football becoming richer, this means that competition has reduced with the bigger teams or richer teams, taking away from the unpredictability. Surprisingly for me, the most unpredictable league during this period 1993-2022, is the Bundesliga. This has now changed in the last 5 years though if you focus just on that. Where is the most predictable league due to Bayern's dominance. One of the supposed draws of the PL is its unpredictability, however over the last 28 years only 6 teams have won the league. This is the same as Germany. The money in the PL has clearly outlined 6 favourites who throughout the book I've described as the 'top 6', in Germany though this is much more reduced, you'd probably say a top 3 or 4 at a push now: Bayern, Dortmund and RB Leipzig, with an additional team then each year rotating to make the CL qualifiers. How it differs is though for the last 8 years, to become 9 this year Bayern have won consecutive leagues, and this has also been done once by Juventus too. In the PL, Man City have now taken over as the dominant force in the league, but of all the Top 5 leagues, Man United are the only team to win 3 in a row two times. Italy and Spain have had 7 winners during the same period. Over 28 years this shows that their is a lack of real chance for most teams to actually win these leagues, this is due to the money that the top teams have compared to their competitors. When you look at the Balon D'or award, 16 out of the 28 awards since the PL began have belonged to Real Madrid and Barcelona. Only two have come from the PL, Michael Owen in 2001 and Ronaldo in 2008. During that period, they have had half of the second and third place finishes. So, Blatter is right, it has become predictable, and this is due to the finances available to these top teams.

The Government are leading a review of fans and how they're treated and changes that are happening to the game in the country. This was being led at the time by Tracey Crouch Conservative MP, who said, "It will look closely at the issues of governance ownership and finance and take the necessary steps to retain the games integrity competitiveness and most important it's bond that clubs have with its supporters and local community's. Behaviour during lockdown, big picture and super league has been a huge own goal."

When we focus on grassroots football, it's important not to forget about how football fans are being treated by clubs and the PL too. Since the PL began pricing of tickets and even TV subscriptions have seen a huge change in England. So not to just seem like this just focussed on the negatives I will start with some positives of the fan experience of the last 30 years. Stadiums are now much more spectator friendly for a start, the Lord Taylor report stated that stadiums should become all-seater stadia, due to the Hillsborough disaster, which has ensured since stadiums have become much safer places. As well as off the pitch, playing surfaces are now much safer and mean the quality of football has improved (some of the pitches on Premier League Years are unbelievable when you look back now, worse than some grassroots). Hooliganism has seen a huge decline; at one point it was unsafe for a family to attend a game due to what would be taking place in the stands and sometimes spilling onto the pitch. Fans now always have instant access to team news for their team or coverage of the league, due to the increased coverage and media access. This is all supplemented by what people would say is also a much higher standard of football on the pitch for fans to watch too, where depending on the team you support or opponent facing you will see some of the world's biggest stars. Lord Taylor report stated that the match day experience of fans had improved.

When looking at the average attendance of PL fixtures, in 1997/98 season the average attendance was 35,000. Compare that to 2019/20 and it now stands at just over 40,000. This shows the league is still sustaining and growing in terms of supporters. However, when you break this down, over 80% of the growth was doing to the increase in capacity of four clubs who had increased their ground size (Liverpool, Tottenham, Arsenal and West Ham). This is one of the reasons that 3 of the above teams have moved stadiums to larger grounds and Everton are doing the same themselves, with an increased capacity and a waiting list of 25,000 season ticket holders. Through these attendance figures it means the PL makes £683m from match day income, which is the most in any league in the world. This is due to however the higher ticket prices seen in the PL and only accounts for 13% of club's incomes, meaning the clubs aren't as reliant on this as other leagues. Success does play a part in increased amount of income, for example when Liverpool won the CL in 2018/19 this saw the club receive £84m in ticket sales, which was an increase on previous years. This was however still behind Manchester United, who due to a bigger ground received £111m from ticket sales (knocked out QF of CL) and Arsenal £96m (didn't qualify for CL, but did reach Europa League final).

When you look at Arsenal for example, ticket prices have rose with the inflation of wages and this is explained as one of the reasons why Arsenal rose ticket prices from the PL start too now. This saw a price rise of average ticket price from £12.50 to £38. This was as the wage bill increased fan example being £10m (start PL) to £83m (95/96). 1995/96 was the first time the wage bill was greater than ticket receipts at 100.9%. This has almost doubled since 2015. However, due to the increased TV revenue, match day revenues have a declining importance on how it affects wage bills. When you look at fans on average and go back further to 1981/82, a UK fan on average wage now must spend 3 times more of the income compared to in those days. The 1992/93 average ticket price at all clubs was £7-8. When you look now using mean and median averages this is around £30, which is a 300% increase. Going back to Liverpool and United, in 1989/90, season ticket price average at Anfield was £60, whilst at Old Trafford it was £96. Looking back to 2010/11 the equivalent tickets were at Anfield £532 and Old Trafford £725. If this was in line with inflation in the UK, then the tickets should've been £106 and £170. Looking at the 2019/20 season, the cheapest season ticket was at Burnley for £325, whilst the most expensive was at Spurs at £1995.

A 2019 EFL survey looked at why fans supported the club they did. Of this 40% respondents identified proximity to where they live. 39% said this was due to family ties. 89% overall match day experience that motivates them to attend. For many like myself, football is like a drug, and it is this which allows us to be taken advantage of. A fan who follows their team home and away will spend 8% of the average UK wage doing this. To compare this 10.6% is spent on average on food and non-alcoholic drink for people on average. So, for some it's either food and drink or football. E-toro found that in 2019/20, supporters who attend matches will spend £1.3b to watch their teams. This is an increase of 31% from 2014/15. Economists describe football fans as being - in elastic demand- suppliers have significant demand to increase price of the goods and services they sell, confident in the knowledge so strong (or essential) is the demand that customers will pay the higher prices. Even if a few buyers are lost the increased prices mean total revenues will be fine, just like smoking for example. The intense supporter demand is what has allowed them to put up ticket prices, knowing fans will still buy and if they don't, the price increase or others in the waiting will take this over. The supporter demand is also what allows them to sell TV subscriptions and see these prices increase too. The demand for football on TV and still retaining the support of fans attending games, is also what allows them to have inconvenient kick off times to suit TV schedules and still know that people will follow this. An example of this being Liverpool travelling to Arsenal on Christmas Eve, but too many others to mention. They also then market new replica stuff throughout the year.

When faced with opposition though and in huge numbers, a difference can be made. The owners of the 'top 6' showed this with the failed Super League idea. It was also shown through organised protests from many clubs to away ticket prices. At the time of the protests in ground by some clubs and supported by marches to the PL Headquarters in 2015, they had also spiralled to see clubs try to take advantage of opposition fans. West Ham had the highest price ticket at £85, whilst their lowest was £25. Arsenal's away tickets ranged from £26 to £64. With Chelsea having their 'cheap' ticket at £47 and their highest at £59, with a much narrower range meaning theirs were probably the worst at the time. All this before you even factor in for an away supported travel and other expenses show it had to stop. Fans protested for 'twenty is plenty' before it was agreed upon this would be a cap of £30 for all away games. This cap on away tickets has also seen most clubs freeze ticket prices for home fans as well, although most home supporters will pay more than that of away fans it is a positive.

One team who did however try to up home ticket prices were Liverpool, who in 2016 tried to up the price of a £59 ticket to £77. This would take season ticket prices for some fans to above £1000 for the first time at Anfield. Once again through protest the owners FSG had to back down, like they also did with the super league. This was done through an organised walkout on 77 minutes, with around 10,000 supporters leaving. FSG responded in the following days saying, "The widespread opposition to this element of the plan has made it clear that we were mistaken." But still that day some fans still had to contend with the "I'm not going to piss on the fire, I'm alright brigade." That day I helped hand out flyers to promote the walkout and was greeted with backlash from some that I should, "support the team". This like you can see with the reaction from some in the public to people striking for a better wage, shows that whatever people do in football, there will be some of those who can afford these rises and don't give a sh*t about the rest. In 2017, the BBC conducted a 'Price of Football' study. In the study, 1000 18–24-year-olds were questioned about attending football. 82% said that the cost of tickets was an obstacle to them attending and watching football. On top of this 65% said the cost of travel was also an obstacle, with 55% saying they could no longer attend due to costs. This shows that the future generations are being priced out of attending football, with it no longer really being a working-class sport for those who attend, but more middle class for those who can afford to attend, with age also increasing with this too. For me personally I was very fortunate that I had parents who would help supplement my tickets or travel but that's not the same for others. It is near impossible for young local lads to support their team anymore and funny enough it wasn't anybody under the age of 40-50, who told me on the day of the 77th minute walkout that I should focus on "supporting the team".

Vincent Kompany did a research project for his Master's in Business at Alliance Manchester Business School. He shared his results in Financial Times to his study in the relationship between atmosphere in stadium and team performance. In his study he concluded PL football should cut ticket prices to allow the right communities to attend football matches. Football must draw a moral line and make sure working-class fans who supported them for generations can afford to go games. In it he found clear links between better home game atmosphere generated by more passionate fans and long-term benefit for all parties.

The study made him wonder whether there's not more value in the premier league as a project by making sure that every single stadium is bouncing for every single game versus trying to squeeze everybody for the last penny... there's an entire business model that stands in the way of even coming near to exploiting home advantage to the maximum. He spoke to 25 current and former players to including Henry and Lampard. The players concluded and agreed that a full stadium with passionate crowd drawn from the local community improved the home team's performance partly by inhibiting the visiting team players. His conclusion was that winning more football matches would be far more beneficial, than putting up prices and therefore leaving some of those from the right communities out of the stadium, they are the people who care. The report therefore found that Germany came out as best stadiums for atmosphere, where fans are treated best. This is summed up perfectly by the quote from former Bayern Munich President Uli Hoeneß. "We could Charge more than €104. Let's say we charged €300. We'd get €2m more income. But what is that to us. In a transfer discussion you argue that sum for five minutes. We don't think fans are like cows you milk." What should highlight to teams the importance of supporters is the results during the COVID hit 2020/21 season. When stadiums were empty, away teams achieve their highest ever success rate in the PL. Atmosphere matters and so do supporters.

Lord Taylor's report didn't propose any financial protection, and this meant fans were able to be exploited. His blind spot was how pay TV would evolve. The PL and clubs didn't intervene, and this meant that fans must subscribe to multiple platforms and prices constantly change. 2019 would see people pay a minimum of £450 for televised TV and often more up to £650 to £700 the way packages are designed. This is a crazy figure when you consider these fans aren't even attending the game and aren't guaranteed to watch all their own teams' fixtures for this price. An example of the greed was during Covid, when the TV companies tried to charge £14.95 per match for games that weren't due to be televised previously. The Times journalist Henry Winter summed it up best in a tweet saying: "£14.95 to watch a game on PPV is disgraceful… it's disgusting. The creed of greed is in PL DNA, but this truly stinks." Once again due to the threat of clubs boycotting these games like some did, during the second lockdown they were offered for free. All this money to potentially must end up watching a game like Stoke and Watford in 2018 in the PL that was a record breaker- the ball was only in play for 42mins of the 96mins and 41 seconds of football.

On top of the prices of tickets and TV, fans have seen the commercial growth of replica kits, in line with that of the clubs they support. For me seeing kids in football kits of different teams is one of the best things you see in grassroots football, but the price of these kits now is taking that away from children too. Many I know can't afford these replica kits and will go to the source and use websites selling 'copies' from Asian manufacturers. The price is even more crazy when you look at adult prices. 20/21 saw a United shirt cost £70, this being the most expensive. United have the highest global appeal in this market, selling on average 1.75m units per year. Whilst the least expensive was Burnley at £45. Clubs now also release new kits every year and this often will be three kits a year. On average in the PL, a home strip will be worn 28 times. The away kit 8 times and of the eleven teams with 3rd kits- these were worn 4 times. Two clubs only wore their away kit on two occasions. This again outlines the greed of clubs that is supported by the demand from fans. Fans without realising it become walking advertisements for the clubs as they wear the clubs' kits and sponsors but are paying huge sums for the pleasure of this

The 20 prem clubs had shirt sponsorship for 19/20 worth £363.6m, analysts sporting intelligence said this was an increase of £80m from the previous year and equivalent to about 50% of match day income. Fans become walking advertisements, yet don't see any of the money being used to allow them to have access to their beloved team for any less. If we look at the last 5 years Ticket price increases had slowed to 1% but this was due to the 16% fall in the capped away tickets. This helped offset any increase to home tickets. During this same period TV subscriptions rose by 41%. Club Merchandising rose also by 21%. Whilst in actual stadiums, Food and beverage rose by 11%. All this is taking place during a cost-of-living crisis. Football is in danger of no longer being accessible to the working-class people of the country and worse stopping many of the younger generation from being able to watch any form of PL football, live ever.

Throughout the book Governance has been shown to be failing football in so many other ways as well. But what are we to expect from individual football associations, when the two biggest governing bodies in football have been proven to be powered by greed themselves, without a second thought for those who love the sport so much.

Bibliography

A Life Too Short: The Tragedy of Robert Enke, by Ronald Reng (Yellow Jersey 2012)

Alex Ferguson: My Autobiography, by Alex Ferguson (Hodder and Stoughton 2013)

An Epic Swindle: 44 Months with a Pair of Cowboys by Brian Reade (Quercus 2012)

Barca: The Rise and Fall of the Club That Built Modern Football, by Simon Kuper (Short Books 2022)

El Diego, by Diego Maradona (Yellow Jersey Press 2005)

Fall of the house of FIFA; How the world of football became corrupt, by David Conn (Yellow Jersey 2018)

Football leaks- Uncovering the Dirty Deals Behind the Beautiful Game, by Rafael Buschmann and Michael Wulzinger (Guardian Faber Publishing 2019)

Hooked: Addiction and the Long Road to Recovery, by Paul Merson (Headline 2022)

Maradona: The Boy. The Rebel. The God, by Guillem Ballague (Weidenfield and Nicolson 2021)

More Than a Game: Saving Football From Itself, by Mark Gregory (Yellow Jersey 2021)

Narcos Inc: the Rise and Fall of the Cali Cartel Book, by Ron Chepesiuk (Maverick House 2017)

No Hunger In Paradise: The Players. The Journey. The dream, by Michael Calvin (Arrow 2018)

Rio: My story with Shaun Custis (Headline 2007)

Roy Keane The Second Half, with Roddy Doyle (Weidenfield and Nicolson 2015)

State Of Play: Under the Skin of the Modern Game, by Michael Calvin (Century 2018)

USA 94- The World Cup That Changed The Game, by Matthew Evans (Pitch Publishing Ltd 2022)

Websites

https://ryanferguson.co.uk

https://www.sportskeeda.com

https://breakingthelines.com

https://thesefootballtimes.co

https://www.sbs.com.au

https://footballiser.com

https://www.goal.com

https://urbanpitch.com

https://boxtoboxfootball.uk

https://mundialmag.com

https://www.theguardian.com

https://bleacherreport.com

https://khelnow.com

https://eu.usatoday.com

https://www.dailymail.co.uk

https://www.statista.com

https://correctiv.org

https://amp.sportsmole.co.uk

https://www.espn.co.uk

https://www.sportingintelligence.com

https://www.mailplus.co.uk

https://www.independent.co.uk

https://thesporting.blog

https://josimarfootball.com

https://www.thenorthernecho.co.uk

https://www.footballbenchmark.com

https://www.mirror.co.uk

https://www.thetimes.co.u

https://www.football365.com

https://www.givemesport.com

https://talksport.com

https://www.skysports.com

https://www.bbc.co.uk

https://www.nytimes.com

https://championhealth.co.uk

https://www.cdc.gov

https://www.samaritans.org

https://www.priorygroup.com

https://www.ons.gov.uk

Printed in Great Britain
by Amazon

18493096R00149